STAND
unashamed

Ellen Harbin

Ellen Harbin

Scriptures marked NIV are taken from the NEW INTERNATIONAL
VERSION (NIV): Scripture taken from THE HOLY BIBLE, NEW
INTERNATIONAL VERSION ®. Copyright© 1973, 1978, 1984, 2011 by
Biblica, Inc.™. Used by permission of Zondervan

Scriptures marked KJV are taken from the KING JAMES VERSION (KJV):
KING JAMES VERSION, public domain.

Printed in the United States of America
First Printing, 2017

ISBN: 10: 1546309276
ISBN-13: 978-1546309277

SLOW Livin' Publishing
Fraser, MI 48026

www.ellenharbin.com

DEDICATION

This book is dedicated to Allen and Linda Schweizer, my dad and mom.

They have been intentionally committed to each other, through
marriage, since 1962. Individually, they have lived unashamed, fully
loving Jesus and wholeheartedly following Him.
It's obvious their joy is complete
as they daily stand firm in their faith, rooted in Jesus.

I love you, dad and mom,
and I'm ever grateful you raised me to know and love Jesus.

CONTENTS

STAND unashamed

Ellen Harbin

ACKNOWLEDGMENTS

I am forever grateful for the people who fill gaps.

Jenny Johnson, serving Jesus alongside you is a joy.
Your creativity and talent as a graphic artist adds to the blessing
of our friendship. Thank you, from the bottom of my heart - for
your constant support, for designing the cover,
and all other graphic art work connected to this project.

A huge shout-out to other gap-fillers:
Joe Cummings -- author photo;
Jerry Cummings – book cover photo;
Mary DeMuth – writing mentor;
Lynne Bucciarelli – editor;
ACCESS prayer team -- Christ Church Fraser, Fraser, MI;
Melena Cummings – always ready with an answer to any
random question in your areas of expertise.

Kevin – doing life with you is never dull. Your devotion and
commitment to our oneness encourages me every day.
Thank you, Babe, for loving me well and cheering me on.
I am, and always will be, devoted to you.

Ellen Harbin

INTRODUCTION

Welcome to the first book of the STAND series, written for you, a woman after God's own heart. Each volume can be read as a book or used for Bible Study. For years I've written and taught Bible Studies, having opportunity to teach many different groups. Women have asked for these studies to be published and others have asked I write to encourage them in their walk with Jesus. The STAND series blends both requests. Each book in this series has a two-word title. The first word will always be STAND.

Isaiah 7:9 says, "...if you do not stand firm in your faith, you will not stand at all." I believe there are too many women stumbling, falling, and crawling as followers of Jesus. I intentionally chose 'STAND unashamed' as the first in this series because I believe shame is a primary contributor to stumbling, falling, and crawling. God never commands we live a certain way and leave us to figure it out. We cannot stand on our strength. We need God, we need Jesus, we need the Holy Spirit to stand firm in our faith.

'STAND unashamed' introduces the reader to some women from the Book of Genesis in the Bible who struggled with shame. These women are no different than women today – we've been deceived to believe shame must be tolerated and accommodated. Those are lies, not truth.

There are obvious shame producing areas in our lives - most from poor choices we've made or others inflicted on us. 'STAND unashamed' tackles ambiguous areas of shame – topics to which no woman is immune. Shame keeps us stuck. Shame hinders our walk with Jesus. Shame messes with our identity in Jesus. As His followers, we belong solely to Jesus, our identity found only in Him.

I love exclamation points. God uses them sparingly, but I caught the one at the end of the declaration in 2Corinthians 5:17. It says, "...if anyone is in Christ, he is a new creation; the old has gone, the new has come!" We are who Jesus says we are. But circumstances occur, shame enters, and identity is skewed. And women stumble, fall, and crawl because shame is a name-changer.

Yes, life is hard. Yes, bad things happen. Yes, we still sin. But those should never change our identity. Shame need not remain because shame isn't your name. Jesus determines identity, not shame. Throughout each chapter KEY POINTS help guide you to stand firm in your faith.

Each chapter ends with four sections for further study and to help facilitate group discussion.

> **PONDER:** deeply, carefully, and thoughtfully consider
> **PERSUADE:** God's Word influences, encourages, and guides
> **PRACTICAL:** applying Biblical Truth to present day
> **PERSONAL:** inviting Jesus into your current reality

Ladies, it's time to name the shame that keeps us from living as Jesus intends. Together we can stand unashamed and firm in our faith.

1

Eve

my name is deceived

Warts. What comes to your mind when you consider these pesky bumps? The first picture that comes to me is the infamous witch from Snow White, the one with a sizeable wart in the center of her nose. It's as if she tilted her head back to expose the visible lump proudly displayed on the center of her face. Even a peripheral view reveals the bump standing like a mini mountain on the slope of her nose.

Until recently I had never been acquainted with warts. Thankfully, my warts were on my fingers and not on the end of my nose. Yet, warts are what will bring clarity to the introduction of the perplexing topic of shame. Yes, warts.

Hang on. I know this seems unlikely, far-fetched, even. Warts and shame. Shame and warts. What could possibly correlate these unrelated entities? However, they share commonalities. Both are pesky, ugly, persistent, and inconvenient. Mutually, they are irritating, bothersome, and frustrating.

As the comparison of these two apparently dissociative words became clear, I had unwittingly allowed an assumption to take root. I had assumed warts were annoyances that only went as deep as the eye could see. Assumptions. Not facts. And in fact, not even the truth.

It took months before I realized what these pesky, ugly, persistent, inconvenient spots were. When they first showed up I presumed they were hangnails simply hanging on. Presumptions. Not facts. And in fact, not even the truth.

Just because you think it, doesn't make it true is a phrase I use to gain proper perspective. I presumed a wart was a hangnail and assumed it wasn't affecting anything deeper than I could see. It wasn't true. Ignored, left unattended and undiagnosed, these spots grew, they turned ugly, they spread. Though small, they brought pain, trouble, and suffering.

Shame is no different. Like a hangnail, shame can be pesky at first. It's assumed inconvenient; therefore, it gets ignored. It's just a nuisance really. However, when shame is left unattended and unnamed it grows, it can turn ugly. When it spreads the whole person gets affected. Pain, trouble, and suffering follow.

Shame has been allowed to run amuck inside your heart and mind affecting your overall relationship with Jesus. Too many of his followers have presumed and assumed that shame must be accommodated and tolerated in their lives.

Presumptions and assumptions. Not truth.

Psalm 25:3 says, "No one whose hope is in you will ever be put to shame." According to God's Word, a woman who trusts in Jesus, whose hope is in the Lord, will never – not once, not ever – be put to shame, as long as she puts her hope in the promises and assurances of the Lord.

For a woman desiring to go deeper in her faith but finds herself stuck; for the woman who knows shame is buried in her heart; for the woman who feels stuck but can't figure out why - they all needs a full and complete understanding of where shame began. And that requires going back to the beginning, to the book of Genesis.

When God designed and created woman, He called her good. This is not only true for Eve - it's true for you and me as well. You are good. Believe it's true, because God says so.

Psalm 102:27 says of God, "you remain the same." And Hebrews 13:8 says of Jesus, "he is the same yesterday, today, and forever."

God doesn't change, he remains the same, so his original design plan for woman has never changed. God made you, he created you, he gave life to you, and he calls you good.

Before shame is introduced, something else must be said.

KEY POINT: WOMAN WAS CREATED WITH NO SHAME

It's true. Eve was good, and she was created to know no

shame. In Genesis 2:25 it says the man and his wife (Eve) were both *naked and they felt no shame.*

Hard to believe? Eve was created shameless. She had no shame. Zero. Zip. None. Eve felt no shame because she was vacant of shame. When she began breathing, shame was non-existent.

I find it interesting that Genesis 2:25 reveals Eve was naked. We understand what this means. Eve didn't. Eve didn't know she was naked. She was a woman who knew perfection; she was living in paradise. Her naked condition was her normal existence.

She hadn't considered if anything was amiss because it wasn't. She didn't care about the size of her nose, she didn't wonder if her hips were too wide. She had no cellulite; she had no spots that didn't belong; she had no warts. I imagine her hair was manageable and her skin flawless. She never had to ask Adam, "Do I look good in this" or "Does my butt look big with nothing covering it?" She felt no shame. She saw nothing wrong with her frame since she was shameless.

Eve was created in God's image. His character was embedded in her. She was kind, helpful, sweet, patient, filled with joy, passionate, willing to work, a good communicator, controlled, respectful, honest, trustworthy, safe, and fun to be with. She knew perfection; therefore, she knew no shame.

She was bare, but she didn't know she was exposed. In order to know shame one must know nakedness, a vulnerability. She was completely uncovered, but she didn't realize anything needed to be covered.

Eve knew no shame. You don't. I don't. We have no idea what it's like to live without shame. We were born into a broken, sin-filled, sinful world. Eve began in paradise. A broken world cannot offer a shameless existence. Eve felt no shame because nothing was broken.

The definition of shame (as a noun), is the painful feeling arising from the consciousness of something dishonorable, improper, ridiculous, etc., done by oneself or another; disgrace; a fact or circumstance bringing disgrace or regret. Eve didn't feel this. She had no idea what dishonor was. Ridiculous was nowhere to be found. Improper was not invited into paradise. She didn't have a clue that shame was even a thing because God designed her to know Him, to trust Him, to live where He dwelled. She knew perfection. She knew no sin. She was without shame.

No other woman has ever lived in a sinless, shameless state or situation. Only Eve. And that's because God placed her in that perfect place. But it only lasted for a time. Eve made a choice, and her choice caused you to be born into a sinful condition. This choice caused a chain reaction that continues today.

In many Bibles, just before Genesis chapter 3, there's a two-word phrase describing how Eve went from a sinless state to a sinful situation.

Two significant words end Genesis chapter two: *no shame*.

Two significant words are used as a subheading to Genesis chapter three: *The Fall*.

Three significant words begin Genesis chapter three: *now the serpent*.

Not all versions of the Bible begin Genesis 3 with the word now, but many do. I like it. Following is, "now the serpent." Now gives me a heads-up that a shift in thought is about to take place. It almost says, "Uh-oh, you better pay attention here." If I were narrating this portion of Scripture, and I was going from chapter two verse twenty-five right into chapter three verse one, I would take a deep breath, exhale, and then say, "now, the serpent..." I may even pause slightly, for effect. There would definitely be a noticeable difference to the inflection of my voice as I said the word now.

The first half of the verse says now the serpent was more crafty than any of the wild animals the Lord God had made. He said to the woman...

KEY POINT: YOU CAN'T PROPERLY INTRODUCE SHAME WITHOUT PROPERLY INTRODUCING SATAN

A new creature is introduced in this verse right in the middle of Eve's perfect place. The serpent. In paradise. Not *a* serpent, but rather *the* serpent. Who is this serpent? What is this serpent? How did this serpent get in the middle of paradise? Why is this serpent talking?

First, this serpent is described as more crafty. The word for crafty here also means shrewd or sly. The use of this word, crafty, means cunning and deceitful. Next, the serpent is described as a wild animal that God made. The Lord God made the serpent. The same God who created all good things is the same God who made the serpent. And we learn this wild animal is the craftiest of all the created creatures.

The devil, Satan, took on the likeness and shape of this wild, crafty animal. Before we move on, we must focus a bit more on Satan. In order to understand why he spoke to Eve, what he said to Eve, and how she responded to him, we must know more about this crafty creature than just his name.

He actually has many names, like Lucifer, Accuser, Adversary, Enemy, Tempter, and Thief. In John 8:44 Jesus has something to say about Satan, "he was a murderer from the beginning, not holding to the truth, for there is not truth in him. When he lies he speaks his native language, for he is a liar and the father of lies." Jesus is clear how he feels about Satan.

Satan contradicts God. Satan is crafty; God is straight up. Satan is not just a liar because he is THE father of lies; God is Truth; and he is our Father. Satan is confusing, a troublemaker, and dwells in chaos; God is concise, a peacemaker, and he abides in order. Jesus, being God, says of Himself, in John 14:6,"I am the way, and the truth, and the life."

Jesus is *THE* way.   Satan is the distracter.

Jesus is *THE* truth.   Satan is the deceiver.

Jesus is *THE* life.   Satan is the destroyer.

Satan is referred to as wicked, which translates to scoundrel or troublemaker. He is shrewd. To be shrewd means to be astute or sharp in practical matters; not necessarily wicked or evil. When acting shrewdly, what's the motive? Satan's motive here in Genesis 3:1 is deception. Satan is crafty. He is cunning. He is shrewd. He is wicked. He is the source of evil.

Evil doesn't just exist or show up. It has a source, a beginning. Satan is evil. He owns it. He operates it. Another name for Satan is the Devil.

I refer to him as Mr. D-evil.

He's still the same today as he was then. He was evil before Eve was created. Jesus said Mr. D-evil has been murdering and lying from the beginning. In John 10:10 Jesus says Satan has come to kill, steal, and destroy. His goal is to kill your will, steal your direction and thoughts, and destroy your motives and perspective. Satan's goal is to deceive you, distract you, and destroy you – it's what he does. It's what he's always done.

Continuing in Genesis 3:1, "he [Mr. D-Evil] said to the woman..."

Wait! Hang on a minute. Picture this in your mind. At this time in history, there is one woman and one man alive on earth. She is the only female on earth. And here she is in paradise, in the perfect place, in her sinless, shameless condition, and a snake starts a conversation with her. A snake speaks. This should have been her hint to bolt! Get out of there, Eve; a snake is speaking to you. But she listens to what the snake has to say.

Genesis 3:1 continues, "...did God really say..."

Throughout history Mr. D-Evil has been quite effective at being crafty, but he hasn't been very creative. The same four words he used to entice Eve are the same four words he uses to distract you. The same four words he used to deceive Eve are the same four words he uses to deceive you. Satan is doing what Satan does best – distracting, deceiving, and destroying.

And yet, *did God really say* is a good and thought-provoking question. There's nothing wrong with this question. God did say some things to Eve and her husband. He gave them boundaries in this perfect place. He shared expectations with them. He didn't leave them unaware of how to live. He provided boundaries to protect them because he loves them. He has some *do's* and *do not's* because he loves them. And because God loved Eve, and her husband, he commanded they were free to eat from any tree in the garden *except* from the tree of the knowledge of good and evil. He told them, he commanded them, not to eat from that one tree. (Genesis 2:16-17)

And because God is a good God and he loves Eve, he even told her why she shouldn't eat from that one tree. *For when you eat of it you will surely die.* When the snake, a.k.a. Satan, Mr. D-evil, asks her this question, *did God really say,* her response was, "we may eat from the trees in the garden, **but God did say** (emphasis mine) you must not eat fruit from the tree in the middle of the garden and you must not touch it or you will die."

God said don't eat, don't touch. And Eve knew the right thing to do. Eve even knew why she shouldn't touch it - she would die, a spiritual death, a separation from God. This would be the worst thing she could know.

I said it before - Eve should have bolted as soon as the serpent started talking. Why? What's the harm in having a conversation with the snake since she knows the truth? Why can't she remain in this conversation with the devil? She responded with truth when confronted with the question, so clearly she can handle herself, right? Before that question gets answered, one more clarification is necessary.

Mr. D-Evil's motive. Remember who's talking right now – the 'father of lies' as Jesus calls him. He's the deceiver, the distractor, the destroyer. Based on these facts alone, what do you think his motive is when talking to Eve? Certainly his motive is not to have a nice, friendly it's-a-beautiful-day-in-the-neighborhood kind of conversation with Eve.

His only motive is to deceive Eve. If he can get her distracted (even just a smidge), then her focus will be on him and her thoughts will be turned toward his misperception. If Satan can get her thinking in a different direction (*distraction*), her feelings guiding her decisions (*destruction*), then she'll begin to question her Creator, listening to Satan's misperceptions, and trusting in her feelings (*deception*). Mr. D-Evil's motivation is to persuade Eve away from the truth.

A woman in an exchange with the devil must be aware that she is substituting safety, security, and shelter for distraction, destruction, and deception. And yet, Eve remains in the exchange.

Genesis 3:4 says, "You will not surely die', the serpent said to the woman..."

Had Eve bolted when a snake appeared, she wouldn't have heard those first four words, *did God really say*, from the Deceiver's mouth. This question grabbed her attention.

KEY POINT: WHATEVER HAS YOUR ATTENTION HAS YOU

My warts had my attention. At times I've been riveted by these pesky bumps. Just look at a picture of the witch from Snow White. Can you look at her face without seeing the wart on the end of her nose?

I learned that these pesky bumps go as deep as they are wide. That had my attention. The discomfort of the warts had my attention. Such little things attempt to disrupt and bring disorder to my life. They had my attention.

Satan has Eve's attention. Eve could have bolted before the question was asked. She could have bolted after those first four words were out of the serpent's mouth. She even had opportunity to bolt after she answered the question.

But Satan has her attention. The Deceiver continues to deceive Eve. Throughout this encounter there are two truths that never changed.

Truth #1 - God loves Eve.

God passionately loves this woman. God still has His eyes on her; He never looked away.

TRUTH #2 – God didn't abandon Eve.

Even though Satan has her attention, God's gaze never left her. He loves Eve so much He can't take His eyes off her.

God loves Eve and has not abandoned her. He allowed Eve to make her own decision. She is not a marionette, connected by strings from heaven for God to control and move where he wants her. He showed her the boundaries and told her what was necessary to enjoy the life he gave her. He is right there in the garden, next to the tree where the serpent has come calling. Just because she doesn't call on God doesn't mean he isn't there. He's prepared to provide her a way out. He has his protection available to rescue her.

Eve had ample opportunity to walk away, to reconsider, to turn her attention back to her Creator. Eve made her choice. She remained. And because she stayed, she gave Satan ample opportunity to show her a different way to think: to question God, rather than trust him.

Satan gets Eve right where he wants her. She has taken a step off her safe foundation, off the path where God had placed her. Mr. D-Evil has averted her attention away from God's words of truth and on to his question of distraction.

KEY POINT: YOU CANNOT HAVE YOUR GAZE IN TWO DIRECTIONS

Hebrews 12:2 urges, "Let us fix our eyes on Jesus..."

Your eyes are to gaze in one direction. On Jesus. The word *fix* in this verse from Hebrews has a two-step meaning. First, take your eyes off something. Second, make your eyes look in a completely different direction. I call this the 'take and make'. Hey, Eve – *take* your eyes off the snake and *make* them gaze on God.

Whatever has your attention has you. Satan had Eve's attention. Therefore, the truth of God, His words, His way, His caution, His commands no longer have her focus. She can't have her eyes completely fixed on God while in a conversation with Satan. The deceiver has Eve distracted. It's what he did, and it's what he still does.

In Genesis 3:5, the deceiving, distracting snake says, "God knows when you eat of it your eyes will be opened and you will be like God."

If Satan can get you distracted, eyes looking and ears listening, then he's accomplished one of his main goals in your life. Eve is no longer leaning on God's truth and trusting His ways. Now Satan has her distracted, listening to and leaning into his deception. The bait is set, and the line is cast. Will she get hooked?

The Tempter has lured Eve. He tempted her to look at the one thing she couldn't have. He deceived her to believe talking with a snake was no big deal. He distracted her to rethink and reconsider what God had told her. Satan twisted God's words. That was part of his deceptive device.

Just because God's words get twisted does not mean they cease being his words. God's words, God's truths, are eternal. His word is flawless (2Samuel 22:31) and perfect (Psalm 19:7-11). They are unchanging (Psalm 119:160). Hebrews 6:18 says, "it is impossible for God to lie."

Seek truth, know truth, trust truth and make the decision to stand on God's truth - no matter what. The Deceiver lurks and desires to distract you. His plans are always to cause destruction on the foundation on which you stand.

Eve knew the truth. She knew the right thing to do and the correct thing to say. But when she chose to remain in a conversation with the serpent, her safety net weakened and she became susceptible to his wicked wiles, as harmless and non-threatening as they appeared.

At this point, Eve has been tempted. No sin has occurred. Like a tightrope walker, Eve teeters on a very thin line, the edge of danger. Satan has just teased her with a new thought: you can be like God. He has Eve focused on the one thing she can't have: the fruit from the one tree that God said to avoid.

The Deceiver has pointed out something that brings a new prospect to Eve. This is the first time she is focused on herself. *What if the snake is right? God wouldn't keep something good from me.* Me. Now her eyes are on herself.

Look out!

Eve hasn't sinned, yet. She has been enticed and tempted. But she hasn't acted on that temptation - yet. However, Satan now has her eyes off God's truth, her ears turned towards his deception, and her focus is on herself. When a woman is focused on herself, sin is not far behind. Isn't it interesting that smack dab in the middle of sin we find an I. s-I-n.

Genesis 3:6 begins, "When the woman saw..."

KEY POINT: OH BE CAREFUL LITTLE EYES WHAT YOU SEE

Eve saw. Satan had her attention, and he knew she wasn't going anywhere. The bait was set, the line was cast, and as soon as she allowed her gaze to graze - she was hooked. She saw. And in an instant, the sin spiral began.

Genesis 3:6 continues, "...she took some and ate it..."

The temper's temptation is now her sin. She looked. She took. She ate. She stopped trusting the voice of truth and turned her ear to the declaration of deception.

Genesis 3:6 concludes, "...she also gave some to her husband who was with her and he ate it."

God created woman to be a suitable helper, a succor. She was designed to help, relieve, aid, support, assist, rescue, and comfort. When a woman stops trusting the voice of God, the voice of truth, other people get affected on the destructive path. Eve took her husband with her. Yes, he is responsible for his own actions, for what Adam did was wrong. Our attention is on Eve. We're not deflecting to Adam. Satan gets Eve distracted, he tempts her, and he deceives her. Now she's sucked into his schemes and cannot be the effective suitable helper she was designed to be.

Instead of being a succor, she was being a life-sucker. Taking other people on your path of destruction is not being helpful to them. Being a succor is life-giving, life-assisting. When Eve took some and ate it, she abandoned Adam, no longer able to be the suitable helper, the aid she was made to be.

Genesis 3:7 begins, "Then the eyes of both of them were opened..."

Open to what? An awareness of something they were never created to know - separation from God. *For when you eat of it you will surely die.* This now her reality: separation from God. Her eyes are opened to her sin. When something falls, it breaks.

Humanity has fallen; they have sinned; they are now broken.

KEY POINT: SIN-TRODUCING SHAME

Genesis 3:7 continues, "...they realized they were naked..."
Shame, this is Eve; Eve, shame. They are now acquainted.
The painful feeling arising from the consciousness of something dishonorable, improper, ridiculous done by oneself or another; a fact or circumstance bringing disgrace or regret is Eve's reality. Shame moved in and deceived her thoughts, distracted her actions, and destroyed her perspective.

All it took was one bite. One distracted gaze + one bite = sin and shame. She refused to bolt, but instead, chose to listen to a voice to which she should never have paid attention, and had her eyes on what she couldn't have. The space in-between *naked and unashamed* and *realized they were naked* is thinner than a piece of sheer fabric. This space of time was quicker than a blink of an eye. It was instantaneous. She bit. She became aware. Bam! Awareness of sin brought an awareness of nakedness. **s-I-n** is now in.

Immediately, Eve is **SIN**-troduced to shame.

Shame is now **IN** her life. Before she looked, before she took, before she was hooked by that bite, Eve had no clue what naked meant. Her eyes were on the things of God: His provision and His words. Now, because she looked, took, and was hooked, where is she focused? On herself. On what she now is, naked. And on what she doesn't have, a cover up. She is no longer focused on God and his truth: she is now focused on her nakedness, which is the result of her sin. Prior to sinning she knew no shame.

Prior to the ugly warts popping out on my fingers I hardly paid attention to my hands. Oh, I'd care for my nails. A little. Once in a while I'd brush a clear polish on them and call it a day. Since those pesky warts have exploded on my digits, my eyes have been opened to some valuable lessons.

Jesus will do that. He uses creative means to get our attention. He had mine. After six months of consistently going to the dermatologist every two weeks, I began to pay attention to the spiritual correlations with my on-going wart dilemma.

The efforts being taken to alleviate the warts appeared ineffective. Appearances are similar to assumptions. Just because it appears one way doesn't make it true. I learned warts are a virus. They deeply embed and take root. Like sin, if not dealt with appropriately, warts will continue to fester and grow. Perseverance and determination kept me going back for continued treatments.

One treatment involved laser. It was explained to me that laser destroys the virus by eliminating the blood supply that keeps it active. An unfed root ceases to produce growth. During the laser treatment I had two unexpected experiences.

Pain and shame.

I'm not ignorant to physical pain. I've had my share over the years. Laser hurts. A lot. I confidently walked into the treatment room ignorant of what was about to occur. I laid on the treatment table experiencing pain that brought uncontrollable tears to my eyes. It caught me off-guard.

So did the shame. I was already somewhat embarrassed by the sight of the warts prior to laser. When blood supply is cut off, it's noticeable. The white-ish, bumpy spots were bad enough but when the black nasty from the laser treatment was added to the already-ugly, it became even uglier.

Three days after the laser treatment I was in church. It was a Sunday. As a congregation we were standing and raising our voices together in song. Occasionally in worship I raise my hands as an expression of praise. On this particular Sunday, as I raised my hands, what immediately followed was quite startling and unexpected. It makes me ponder what Eve experienced as she was startled by her nakedness.

Eve was shocked by her nakedness when shame entered her world. She is experiencing an inner painful feeling because she knows she did wrong. She knows. She's aware. Because she's smart? No. Because God loves her and has revealed this painful feeling inside her consciousness. He said he would. *If you eat of it, you will surely die*. She's died. Not physically, though that will now be in her future. Spiritually she's dead. There's a gap, a chasm, between her and her Creator.

That gap or chasm, that separation from God, is sin. Sin separates. Sin devastates. And shame is like its Siamese twin. Sin and shame are cohorts, closely connected accomplices. Sin is the leader and shame follows. Eve's sin is exposed, and she realizes she's naked. We must uncover her response.

KEY POINT: SHAME CREATES A COVER-UP

Genesis 3:7 goes on, "...so they sewed fig leaves together and made coverings for themselves."

Her mess-up made her believe she needed a cover-up. How ironic. The sarong, a garment made of flowing fabric that conceals a bathing suit, is a cover-up. A bathing suit covers up nakedness, and the cover-up covers up what already was covered up.

Eve donned the first cover-up in history. However, the fig leaves will not cover-up what she thinks needs to be covered up. A shadow of shame has been cast over her heart from the sin that entered her life. This shadow of shame startled Eve, and she reacted by covering up.

I, too, was shocked. By warts. Yup, those same pesky, bumpy, ugly blemishes on my hands reminded me of the ugly blemish of shame on Eve's heart. While singing and worshiping that Sunday after the laser treatment on my warts, I raised my hands in worship. What happened next caused a commotion of emotion in my heart. I became more aware of my hands than Jesus. Like the tall 'I' in the middle of sIn - I had my attention. Jesus was no longer my focus. As I raised my hands in praise, the dark spots on my thumbs suddenly appeared larger than the thumb itself.

One second my hands were raised in praise, and the next moment shame took over. My hands shot down by my sides quicker than they had gone up. Oh, I kept on singing. But those warts on my hands had my attention. I was embarrassed, ashamed of warts. And I hid. I hid my hands out of sight, ashamed they would be seen.

Genesis 3:8 states Eve hides from the Lord. Her first response when sin and shame enter her life is to hide...from God. God is omnipresent; he's present in all places at all times. It's almost ludicrous that Eve thinks or attempts to hide from an all-seeing, all-knowing, ever-present God. But shame will do that. Shame's dark shadow hid in her heart, and she's hiding from God. He didn't cause the shame; shame is the result of her sin. Hiding is the result of the shame now hidden in her heart.

But God still loves Eve. And he proves it.

Genesis 3:9 says, "but the Lord God called to the man [and woman]" [emphasis mine]

Who pursues whom? The Lord God pursues Eve. Love pursues. Shame made her hide. Shame made her cover up. And God still initiates contact with her; he calls out to her.

Genesis 3:9 records, "God calls, 'where are you?'"

Not only is God omnipresent, ever-present, but he is also omniscient, all-knowing. God knows everything. Then why does he ask *where are you*? God is giving Eve a chance to respond to his voice. She knows God's voice, so she would recognize it. Satan has just distracted her, deceived her, and destroyed the closeness she had to God, causing a separation that confuses her. Eve's emotions are chaotic, and they are in charge of her actions.

God pursues her, and he desires to restore her. First, He must get through and uncover the shame that has been cast. God does not want her living in shame so he calls out to her.

If a woman doesn't deal with shame correctly, then it will definitely deal with her. She will be at risk of being emotionally harried, mentally messy, and spiritually unsettled. When shame is in control, her life will be out-of-control.

There's good news for a woman whose heart belongs to Jesus. He meets you at the edge of your hiding place, calls to you, bids you to come out, and sheds light on the shadow revealing shame that has caused you to cover up and hide.

KEY POINT: FACE YOUR SHAME

Facing shame demands honesty. It requires a steadfast trust in Jesus who's willing to uncover the shadows that hide in your heart. Facing your shame requires coming face-to-face with Jesus. God's passionate pursuit of you proves He first loved you. First John 4:19 says He first loved us. This ever-present, always-has-been love strengthens and helps us face shame.

Eve doesn't face her shame well. She's been distracted and deceived, her paradise is destroyed, and now she deflects from facing the truth of what happened. Eve's eyes are still on herself. When a woman has her eyes on herself, she can't have them fully on Jesus and respond to him in a face-to-face encounter. God initiates this face-to-face with Eve, but she's still focused on her circumstances rather than the one who first loved her.

Deflecting responsibility casts blame. Instead of facing the shame, you begin casting blame which casts more shadows of shame on a heart. It's a vicious cycle.

Eve becomes a willing participant in the first ever Shame Game. We see this game of blame played out in Genesis 3:11-13.

God to Adam: "Have you eaten from the tree that I commanded you not to eat from?"

Adam to God: "The woman you put here with me gave me some...and I ate it."

Adam blames God. Adam blames Eve. Adam deflects *then* Adam admits.

God to Eve: "What is this you have done?"

Eve to God: "The serpent deceived me, and I ate."

Eve blames Satan: the serpent deceived me (a.k.a. the devil made me do it.) Then she admits. *After* she deflected by blaming the snake. Deflection is casting blame.

Let's be clear. God is not a participant in this man-made game of shame and blame. God questions his children, not because He is ignorant and uninformed, but because he desires they take responsibility for their actions.

He is helping Eve to face the shame in her heart with honesty. However, she is attempting to justify her actions which deflects away from responsibility and gives shame ample opportunity to take up residence in the hidden places of her heart. These remnants of shame remain hidden, accommodated in a heart. Women are then deceived to believe this hidden shame must be tolerated and end up stuck on their faith journey.

In His passionate pursuit of your heart, Jesus shines His light at the edge of hidden shame. The Light of the World removes the shadows and reveals the hidden places allowing you to face the shame that keep you from living as he intends. Face Jesus, and He'll help you face the shame.

That Sunday, as I was singing praises to Jesus, with my hands hanging down by my sides hiding the warts that caused me shame, I heard a voice ask me a question. The same question asked of Eve was the same question asked of me. *What is this you have done?*

Hanging in the front of the sanctuary is the emblem of suffering and shame. The cross is the ultimate sign of God's love. Romans 5:8 says, "But God demonstrates His own love for us in this: while we were still sinners Christ died for us." Jesus hung on the cross. God demonstrates His love for me. Jesus died on the cross. God demonstrates His love for me. Jesus had wounds in His hands for me. He suffered for me. He spread His arms wide as the nails were pounded into His hands. For me. Every pound of the nail meant freedom from guilt. Every pound of the nail meant freedom from shame.

As I was gazing at the cross where my Savior hung to take away my sin and shame, my hands were hanging by my side ashamed. Jesus had me in a face-to-face encounter. *What is this you have done?* I flung my hands back up in praise of Jesus, my Savior, for what he had done for me. I lifted my hands to the one who gave his life for me. The shame from the warts no longer had my attention...Jesus did.

The scars on Jesus' hands are still visible. His scars haven't disappeared. He bears the scars to remind us of God's deep, pursuing, passionate love. His scars go deep because his arms went wide.

When I was a little girl we sang a song in church, a simple song called Deep and Wide. The lyrics are repetitive so that the message is clear. The love of Jesus is deep. His love will reach to the deepest sin. The love of Jesus is wide. His arms were spread wide on His cross making His love wrap around the widest shame. His scars are deep, and His love is wide.

Perhaps you've been deceived, like Eve, to believe you must make room for shame in your heart. If this is true, then please listen to Jesus. He will not deceive you. Shame was nailed to the cross, along with your sin. It sounds rather uncomplicated, doesn't it? That's because it is. Your heart knows chaos because you've been deceived to believe that it must be accommodated. Your heart knows confusion because you've been deceived to believe that it must be tolerated.

It is time Christian women stop accommodating and tolerating obscure areas of shame in their hearts. Your heart is not Satan's playground – your heart belongs to Jesus, and the shadows of shame hidden in your soul no longer need to keep you stuck on your faith journey.

Living as Jesus intended is shameless because He says so.

PONDER

deeply, carefully, and thoughtfully consider

1. Woman was created to be shameless. Does this fact hinder or help you to better understand shame?

2. *Whatever has your attention has you* – consider how Satan distracts and deceives.

3. Describe a time when shame caused you to hide from an omnipresent [everywhere] and omniscient [all-knowing] God.

PERSUADE

God's Word influences, encourages, and guides

1. Read John 8:44. How does Jesus' description influence your awareness of Satan?

   Read John 14:6 How has Jesus persuaded you to believe He is who He says He is?

2. What four words did Satan speak to Eve?

   Genesis 3:1 _____

   How does Satan use these same words to dissuade you?

3. Read Hebrews 12:2. The word *fix* means to first take your eyes off something followed by making your eyes look in a completely different direction. How does this encourage you that shame no longer needs to be accommodated and tolerated?

PRACTICAL
applying Biblical Truth to present day

1. When Satan tempted Eve, she was distracted. Discuss a time when your eyes were off God's ways and gazing in a different direction. What resulted?

2. *I* stands tall in the middle of sIn. Discuss what this means and how it's related to shame.

3. God pursued Eve. He always initiates. How has He pursued you? How have you responded?

4. What benefit is there in facing shame vs. participating in the blame game?

PERSONAL
inviting Jesus into your current reality

1. What life lessons did you learn from Eve on how to stand unashamed? How will you apply them to your current reality?

2
Sarai
my name is half-hearted

When I was 12 my family vacationed at a cabin on a lake. Other families were there doing the same thing. All kids immediately bonded as if we'd been friends for life. Every night was a repeat of the night before, wait until dark and let the game begin. The game of choice was Kick-the-Can. Someone is declared 'it' and mans the can. Everyone else scatters and hides. The one manning the can is to 'catch' everyone who is hiding. If they're caught, they congregate at the can. All those not caught attempt to sneak up on the can and kick it (yes, whoever named this game was a creative one) which frees anyone who has been caught. (If you haven't heard of this game, you'll want to do research on the official rules since I'm only giving a brief understanding to help my story.)

Assuming you're still with me, I was a scattered one hiding. One particular girl and I always stayed together. It was her turn to be the leader of our twosome and find us good hiding spots, and I would follow her no matter what. Great plan. Halfhearted following would get me caught and I didn't want that, so I wholeheartedly followed my friend.

Caught! The one manning the can decided to aggressively run after all the ones attempting to hide. He set his sights on my friend and me. Angela began running as fast as those short legs on her 4'10" frame could go. All 5'7" of me was on her heels. After all, I was following her no matter what, remember? Her plan was to quickly weave around the cabins that were closely positioned to each other. We turned a corner. BAM!

One second I was running as fast as I could, wholeheartedly following my leader, and the next I was lying on the ground, stunned. As I got up (yes, the man of the can tagged me as well)

I immediately recognized the pain coming from my face.

It didn't take any investigative skill to put the pieces together. You see, Angela's 4'10" frame fit nicely under the clothesline attached between the cabins. She kept running, but as I followed I was brought down as the rope attached to the cabins attached to my mouth. Apparently, as I wholeheartedly followed, I was also screaming as a 12-year-old would. My opened mouth was used to stop any forward progress on my part. For days it looked like I had taken a huge bite from the center of a grape jelly sandwich. Two purple lined bruises jutted out from the corners of my mouth and across my cheeks, as a reminder of what had stopped me from following.

There will be times when you are following Jesus wholeheartedly and you'll run into something that can potentially bring you down. Sarai knows this to be true. You may know her as Sarah. Sarai is her birth name. God later changed her name to Sarah (more on her in chapter 4.) Sarai is a woman who teaches us how to follow God with your whole heart. She is also a woman who flailed, floundered, as a halfhearted follower of God.

Following means to accept the authority of a leader; to imitate, to copy, to obey. The implication must be mentioned: followers require a leader. When children play follow-the-leader, the game is only effective if there's one leader and everyone else follows. Otherwise, chaos erupts.

Leaders lead. Followers follow. Followers have a responsibility to make sure they know who they're following, why they're following, and if they're effective at following.

As a licensed driver, you are a follower. There are rules, laws to follow, to obey. There are the drivers who choose to follow the rules, the law. And there are drivers who *think* they only need to follow the rules and the laws that they determine only apply to them. If this concept of picking and choosing which rules you want to follow is transferred to your spiritual life, then there are some very frustrated followers of Jesus who are flailing, and perhaps even failing. Believers in Jesus, disciples of Jesus, cannot pick and choose certain rules, commands, laws, statutes, or precepts and only follow them.

KEY POINT: FOLLOWING GOD MEANS FOLLOWING ALL HIS WAYS

• Reading God's Word will change your life – if you choose to follow it.

• Reading the Bible will challenge your actions, your thoughts, your motives – if you choose to follow it.

• The Lord God provided His word so you could know the author personally, love the author deeply, and follow Him more closely – if you choose to read it.

Drivers who change the law to fit their individual circumstance are, well, they're wrong. A follower of Jesus is no different. If she thinks she can rewrite His rules, ignore His laws, turn a blind eye to certain behavior, she's wrong. Wholehearted followers of Jesus follow at all times, not only when it's convenient, or if it makes them look good or benefits them, but all the time.

I love that God uses real people in real situations to tell a real story that we can learn from and apply to our current realities. Sarai is one of these real people. She followed, and she flailed. She was a wholehearted follower who got stuck on her faith journey and flailed, becoming a halfhearted frustrated follower. When Sarai flailed, shadows of shame were set in her heart. God desires we learn from Sarai's hidden shame of halfhearted following.

Genesis 12:1 begins, "The Lord had said to Abram..."
God is involved in people's lives. The Lord, Jehovah, the name used here for God, *had said* **to** Abram. (Just like his wife, Abraham had his name changed – his birth name was Abram.) Jehovah speaks *to* Abram. The one, true God takes time to pay attention to one man. The Lord chose this very moment to speak *to* Abram. God initiates this connection. God establishes his leadership over Abram and desires Abram be the follower.

Jehovah initiates relationship with you as well. He loves you. He pays attention to you as well. He has something to say to you just like he did Abram. Our God is a relational God. He chooses to relate, to connect, to interact with you. God desires to be your exclusive leader. That makes me excited. That makes my heart leap. I about jump out of my skin at the thought of God paying attention to you and me. He loves you so much he chooses to interact with you and desires to lead you. Are you moved by this fact?

God is always the initiator in a relationship with Him. In Genesis 12:1, the Lord speaks to Abram. Genesis 11:29 tells us Abram is Sarai's husband. What God had to say to Abram, God also intended for his wife, Sarai.

Digging in deep to the story of Abram and Sarai is crucial to fully comprehending how to live as wholehearted followers of Jesus.

In Genesis 12:1, it says," ...Leave..."

God is speaking to Abram, but Sarai is involved. The first word she hears is *leave*.

KEY POINT: DON'T PLUG YOUR EARS IF THE MESSAGE IS OVERWHELMING

Leave. Really? Leave and go where? All too often followers of Jesus get stuck on *what* is being said rather than on *who* is doing the speaking. Perhaps the Lord has one word for you as well. Have you listened? Or are you stuck on the word instead of following the leader? Like little children do you have your fingers plugging your ears saying *la-la-la-la, I can't hear you*?

Sarai's word was *leave*; what's yours? Forgive? Wait? Stop? Trust? Go? Repent? Return? Love? What's the one word God is speaking to you?

Does the word overwhelm you, or are you overwhelmed that the Lord has something to say to you? Sarai, along with Abram, listens to God. She is a faithful follower even when God speaks a challenging word. She remained right where she was and listened beyond the one word.

Genesis 12:1 goes on, "...leave your country, your people, your father's household..."

Leave what's comfortable. Leave your town. Leave your extended family. Leave your friends. Leave the place you call home. Leave what you know. Leave your security. Leave your comfort zone. Leave. Remember this is God's plan for Sarai. Your plan is tailor-made for you. What's your one word?

In Genesis 12:1 God keeps talking, "...and go..."

Leave and go. How does a woman hear *leave and go* and not have a follow-up question? A woman who follows wholeheartedly doesn't *need* more information, but if God chooses to give more, that's His prerogative.

" ...go to the land I will show you."

My paraphrase: Sarai, start walking, and I'll tell you when to stop.

KEY POINT: WALK BY FAITH NOT BY SIGHT

Second Corinthians 5:7 clearly says, "We live by faith not by sight."

To live by faith, or to walk by faith, literally means to *regulate your life* by faith. Wholehearted followers of Jesus are to regulate their lives to His ways. God speaks one word to you. Are you prepared to remain and hear more of what He has to say? Regardless of how impossible, radical, crazy, or unimaginable it seems, are you ready to listen? Regulating your life to His ways and to His purposes allows you to stay and listen to more of what He has to say.

The geographical *leave and go* call from the Lord is uncommon. More frequently, Jesus is heard saying *leave your life of sin and go and sin no more*. Followers of Jesus hear *leave* that bad habit, or *leave* your bad attitude, or *leave* that character flaw.

God spoke the *leave and go* to my husband Kevin in 1993. God called Kevin to be a pastor. *Leave*? (Walk away from our careers, our well-paying jobs, the newly purchased house, pregnant with our third child in three years, our church, our friends, our family?) *Now*? (and move to another state while Kevin attends seminary?) *You can't be serious*. Yes, those words formed in my brain, landed on my heart, fell out of my mouth, and into the ears of a woman who follows Jesus with her whole heart.

After hearing about my attitude (apparently I hadn't kept that tamped down), she called and said she had a question for me. "Ellen, someday God is going to ask you why you derailed the plan he had for you and Kevin. How will you respond?" Well. Eh-hmmm.

I immediately went to Kevin and told him I was all-in on the *leave and go* plan God had for us. The thought of having to face my Lord and give an answer to that question catapulted me to regulate my life to God's ways, walking by faith. I was back to wholehearted following.

The same thing happened with Sarai hundreds of years earlier. She started walking by faith, and regulating her life to God's ways, walking by faith, following Him every step of the way.

Walking by faith recognizes that not only is God the initiator of your relationship with Him, but He also initiates any assignment assigned for you. When God came to Sarai and her husband with the call to leave and go, her heart was prepared to listen to the call, to accept this call, to willingly follow the call, then to begin walking by faith.

God prepared her heart to hear what He had to say, and He'll continue to give her all she needs on the journey as long as she continues to wholeheartedly walk by faith. In Genesis 12:2-3 God reveals what he will do as they follow his ways. I call these the *Seven I Wills*. God will…
- show you where to go
- make you into a great nation
- bless you
- make your name great
- bless those who bless you
- curse those who curse you
- cause all peoples on earth to be blessed through you

As a keeper of His word God is ready to do all these thing as long as Sarai chooses to wholeheartedly walk in obedience completely trusting God.

KEY POINT: HAVE AN UNWAVERING TRUST IN THE LORD

Sarai could trust the call on her life because she could trust the One who's calling. As a follower, she could trust the one who is leading. She didn't know how to leave her home, her family, her friends - she'd never done that before. You must be resolved that God doesn't wait for you to be completely prepared before He calls you to whatever task He has planned for you. Wholehearted following can mean you get prepared as you go.

Trusting the Lord when He speaks to you is part of the preparation required for whatever journey, or one-word command, he has for you. Sarai had a complete faith and trust in the Lord as he told her to leave. How do we know this?

Genesis 12:4-5 tells us, "So Abram left...he took his wife Sarai..."

Sarai did not sign up for all the conferences on *how-to-follow-God-when-He-calls*; she did not take the time to read a book titled, *God Called; Now What?* She did not have coffee with her best friends and gain their opinion. She did not negotiate or compromise with God.

Prior to the phone call where I was asked that question that snapped me back to wholehearted following, I had been negotiating with God. Originally I was immediately on board with Kevin going to seminary. I recall going for a walk with Kevin while pushing the double stroller filled with our two children under the age of two. We were having a conversation about adding two more children to our family but waiting until after he graduated from seminary and settled in our first church. That was our six-year plan. That was me negotiating with God.

I wasted time, emotions, words, and unnecessary brain space on that negotiation. Unbeknownst to us, I was already pregnant with our third child. The next day I had something weird happen (I'll spare you the details), and it made me purchase a pregnancy test. I won't spare this detail: I immediately stopped taking the ineffective birth control pills.

Let the negotiation continue. *Now that I'm pregnant, which by the way, God, it would have been nice to know earlier, how about we wait a few years before Kevin begins seminary?* I was on a slippery slope expecting God to see my predicament and compromise his original plan. That's halfhearted following. *Oh, I'll still leave and go, I'm good with that.* Just not right now.

A woman with an unwavering trust in God follows with her whole heart. The Lord directed Abram and Sarai, and they followed. They didn't ask *are you sure*; they didn't ask *how*; they didn't say *you've got to be kidding*; they didn't say *I'll do it only if*; they simply obeyed. And they left. No negotiating.

So Abram left could be translated *so they began walking by faith* or *they started faithfully following God* or *their lives were regulated by God's will and His way*. Sarai has an unwavering trust in God. She's ready to follow God with her whole heart, with no idea where the next step will take her. And she's ok with that.

Sarai didn't have a mini-van to pack. They didn't rent a U-Haul. They didn't buy a travel trailer or a bus. They loaded up the camels with all the possessions they had accumulated since being married, prepared the people who worked for them, and as Genesis 12:5 says, "...they set out and arrived."

When a follower of Jesus faithfully follows the Lord with her whole heart, she will always arrive where He leads, as long as she follows His lead. Age is not a restriction when God has a plan. No one is too young or too old to be given an assignment by God.

Sarai was 65 years old and her husband was 75 when they began this new journey of walking by faith, not by sight. Sarai was a 65-year-old wholehearted follower. Do not miss this. Sarai didn't delay from God's call with excuses like *I'm too old* or *I'm set in my ways* or *I'll never be able to do that*. A wholehearted follower faithfully follows. Period. No excuses, no delays.

Genesis 12:7 records, "The Lord appeared to Abram and

said, 'to your offspring I will give this land'..."

The Lord chose to appear to Abram, and Abram chose to pay attention when the Lord appeared. God says something intense, perhaps even overwhelming for Sarai and Abram to comprehend. This couple has faithfully followed God. They have wholeheartedly walked by faith and not by sight. And God decides to share more of his plan with these followers. He said he would give them *this* land. The land they were standing on, walking on, living on would one day belong to their offspring.

That's intense. That's an overwhelming statement of promise. In Genesis 11:30 it states that Sarai was barren; she had no children. I was a 29-year-old woman when I was surprisingly pregnant with child #3. I was overwhelmed. Sarai is a 65-year-old woman, and she has just heard that her offspring would own the land on which they're currently standing. Offspring would require Sarai to deliver a child. But Sarai is barren. Sarai is unable to become pregnant. AND SHE'S 65 YEARS OLD!

What?!? Is this some sick joke? Sarai chooses to walk by faith on this *leave and go* plan, regulating her life to the promises and will of Almighty God. She leaves her family, her friends, and her comfort zone and moves to a faraway place. That's intense and overwhelming all on its own. And now she hears that at 65 God has a plan to give this land to her offspring - to the children she's unable to conceive.

This doesn't make sense.

KEY POINT: WHOLEHEARTED FOLLOWING DOESN'T ALWAYS MAKE SENSE

Sarai and her husband kept following, they kept walking by faith, regulating their lives to God's call and His plan for them, even when God's ways became intense. Even when His words didn't make sense. Even then, Sarai faithfully followed her leader, God. The response they had is proof of their wholehearted devotion even when things didn't make sense. In Genesis 12:7-8 it states they built an altar to the Lord.

Wholehearted followers of Jesus are aware that God may say something intense. He might not make sense. What he has to say may be overwhelming or confusing and may even seem extreme. What Sarai just heard could potentially baffle and perplex her. But that didn't stop her from responding as a wholehearted follower.

KEY POINT: LIVES ARE ALTERED AT THE ALTAR

Sarai and Abram built an altar to the Lord. Wholehearted followers of Jesus will only have their lives altered if they abide at the altar. Though Abram literally built an altar to the Lord, you don't need to physically build one to remain at one. The significance doesn't come from the structure itself. Abiding at the altar focuses on who does the altering. Abram built an altar, and he and Sarai must abide at the altar. God will alter Sarai's heart so she can continue to wholeheartedly follow.

You'll notice since the beginning of this chapter shame has not been mentioned. It has not been associated with Sarai. That's because a wholehearted follower is an unashamed follower. Sarai chose to follow closely, she chose to remain at the altar, she chose to follow God's ways and she walked by faith. Shame won't land on a heart when a woman is wholeheartedly following God.

God is still leading. He is a keeper of His word. He told Sarai and her husband that He would do some amazing things if they faithfully followed. God's eye has never left Sarai. His watchful eye has never left her because God will never call you to a task, or an assignment and then leave you stranded. Whatever your one word is from God, He doesn't abandon you while waiting to see if you'll obey. He doesn't turn away from you once He's spoken the word.

What is your word? Is it *stop*? Perhaps you've doubted and he says *stop*. Perhaps your attitude toward another has been unacceptable, and he says *stop*. You participate in gossip, you're reading books you shouldn't, you spend too much money, you yell too much, you watch too much TV, you worry, you cuss, you're snippy or snotty – God says, *stop*. His eye is on you before you hear His voice, as you hear His voice, and as He waits for you to obey His voice. Will you wholeheartedly listen and obey, or will you halfheartedly give it consideration?

KEY POINT: DO NOT TAKE YOUR EYES OFF JESUS

Now. If you recall, this three letter word began Genesis chapter three and hinted that something was about to happen. Here in Genesis 12:10 this same small word makes a comeback and implies something big is about to take place. If I were to paraphrase this verse, I would insert *UH-OH* for the word *now*. Uh-oh conveys what *now* is about to communicate.

Genesis 12:10begins, "UH-OH [now] there was a famine in the land."

Uh-oh, a famine. Uh-oh, hard times. Uh-oh, a crisis. STOP!!

An unashamed, wholehearted follower of Jesus needs to stop and consider what will have her attention. Remember *whatever has your attention has you*. A wholehearted follower fixes her eyes on Jesus. He has her attention. The half-hearted follower is focused on the famine. And she is at risk of flailing or even failing as a follower.

God led Sarai right to where He wanted her. Wait. God led them into trouble? He walked them right into a famine? They choose to follow Him, to regulate their lives to His leading, His way, and He leads His unashamed, wholehearted followers right into a crisis? That's called leading?

Inquiring whether God led them straight into trouble or implying that God abandoned her now that a famine is present focuses on the famine. And this is where the risk of flailing takes root.

God still has His eye on Sarai. He hasn't abandoned her. She would know this if she wasn't focused on the famine. God didn't cause this particular famine, but He certainly allowed it. His followers can be assured He's still leading and guiding and directing in spite of the famine. Trouble and crisis do not interrupt God from keeping His promises. However, just because God is leading doesn't mean His followers are still following.

They aren't. Abram and Sarai ceased wholeheartedly following God. She is now a halfhearted follower. Abram takes Sarai down to Egypt to live there for a while due to the severe famine.

Genesis 12:11-13 says, "Abram is about to enter Egypt and he says to his wife, 'I know what a beautiful woman you are and when the Egyptians see you are my wife they'll kill me and let you live. Say you are my sister, I will be treated well and my life spared."

Sarai's focus is now on Egypt. Some think Abram is a stand-up guy here: providing for his wife, making a plan before entering a place where his life is in danger, and making sure to protect Sarai by creating a diversion and saying she's his sister. Just because you think it doesn't make it true. The fact is, Abram is about to walk his wife right into jeopardy, danger, and possible peril.

As their leader, God has their provision, their plan, and their protection taken care of – He didn't ask for their help, but wanted their trust and their obedience. Wholehearted followers trust and obey. Halfhearted followers flail creating their own procedures.

Sarai is now wavering between following and failing, she's flailing.

Halfhearted following casts shadows of shame on a heart...shadows of half-hearted joy, half-hearted peace, half-hearted passion. Doubt, anxiety, guilt, identity crises, depression, unmet expectations, and more threaten to take up residence in those hidden places left vacant when wavering from wholehearted following.

When a wholehearted follower focuses on a famine (trouble, crisis, hard times) instead of being controlled by God, she begins to flail as a follower and quickly finds life spinning out of control. Sarai flailed by taking matters into her own hands, ignoring God's promises, and straying away from his ways.

KEY POINT: DON'T STRAY – STAY, FOLLOW GOD'S WAY

Sarai should have stayed; instead she strayed. Joshua 1:5 says, "I will never leave you or forsake you." God called Sarai to leave, but He will never leave Sarai. She wavered on this truth and got stuck as a halfhearted follower on her faith journey.

God made certain promises to Sarai, but he never promised an easy journey. He never implied her life would be comfortable, but he inferred she should trust him, no matter what. When God promised all that land, Egypt was not a part of the promised land. God's way said stay. Sarai's way made her stray.

In Proverbs 3:5-6 it says, "Trust in the Lord with all your heart and lean not on your own understanding. In all your ways acknowledge Him and He will make your paths straight."

God had a straight path prepared for them; Abram and Sarai strayed on a self-made course. They assumed a famine was not a part of God's straight path for them. They went from walking by faith to walking by sight, taking matters into their own hands. God's way was stay. Their way was stray. God's way has no shame. Their way brings shame.

Kevin and I and our three children made it to where he would attend seminary. We quit our jobs, sold our house, loaded up the U-Haul, and drove 350 miles following where God led. If you were to ask me at that time if I was a wholehearted follower, I would have looked you square in the eye and answered a resounding yes. But internally I was flailing. How does a wanna-be pastor's wife admit she's a flail-ure?

The truth is, half-hearted was a more accurate description. On the outside looking in I had it all together. Kevin studied to be a pastor while working three part-time jobs, and I was a stay-at-home mom with baby #4 arriving 16 months after our arrival to this new land. Finances were tight, as were our living quarters. The six of us lived in 800 square feet, but we appeared content.

I was not content. I was a frustrated, flailing follower. Why? The obvious answer was this: I wasn't following wholeheartedly. The reason for the flail-ure is that I needed to deal with some hidden places in my heart. This shame needed exposure to Jesus.

How did I know these areas needed to be revealed? Behind the closed doors of that 800 square foot townhouse was a chasm of discontent that showed up in an impatient, argumentative, frustrated, going-through-the-spiritual-motions, uptight, flailing follower named Ellen. The shadows of shame kept me from following Jesus with my whole heart.

Abram and Sarai strayed to Egypt on their self-guided tour. Before they enter Egypt Abram tells his barren wife she must lie to the Egyptians. Apparently Sarai is a very beautiful 65-year-old lady and they'll want to kill him and add her to the Pharaoh's harem. Walking by sight leaves room for shame to invade Sarai. Abram's plan is for them to lie. They're to say Sarai is Abram's sister. Genealogy facts say they share the same father. Marrying within your bloodline was acceptable back then. Technically, it's not a lie that they're half-siblings. What about motive?

What was the motive for disclosing this information? Wholehearted followers of Jesus deal in truth at all times. Truth is absolute. Something either is true or it isn't. There is no such thing as a half-truth. The only time their blood connection is mentioned is through deception. These half-siblings tell a half-truth causing their half-hearted devotion to God.

The day Abram and Sarai were joined together in marriage they were on God's leave and cleave plan. They each left their respective families and a new family began. I now pronounce you Mr. and Mrs. Abram was the truth. Abram left and cleaved to his wife Sarai, not his half-sister.

Walking by sight failed these followers and caused their deception to bring deflection away from the truth.

Their lie appears to work. Genesis 12:14-16 says Pharaoh brought Sarai into his palace, and Abram was treated well for her sake. He was given sheep, cattle, donkeys, menservants, maidservants, and camels. Yay!! It worked. A famine may be brewing and stewing where they used to be, but down here in Egypt they're now rich! They acquired more than they hoped for. What's so wrong with telling a half-truth?

Carefully read Genesis 12:9-16. Is the Lord mentioned? Not once. Does Abram inquire of the Lord? Not once. In 12:7 and 12:8 Abram builds altars to the Lord as soon as he landed in those particular places. God led them there, He met them there, and Abram built altars to Him there. But in Egypt, while walking by sight, Abram and Sarai were too distracted to consider the Lord. From the time Abram and Sarai left their second altar, experienced famine, strayed to Egypt, deceived the Egyptians, and stayed in Egypt there is no recording of an altar being built anywhere.

As a flailing follower I had something in common with Sarai. I didn't abide at the altar either. My relationship with Jesus was on my terms. I went to church, I went to Bible study, I listened to Christian radio, read Christian books, sang in the church and seminary choirs, and served on a leadership team ministering to other women whose husbands were seminary students. I was doing so much in the name of Jesus that I didn't spend any time with Jesus.

I was avoiding time at the altar. More vital than meeting Jesus at the altar is Jesus altering you at the altar. And I had some deep altering that needed to take place. It's funny...we loaded up that U-Haul and moved 350 miles away, and I brought baggage I hadn't remembered packing - baggage that Jesus needed to go through. Baggage that was hidden in my heart with a shadow keeping the shame blocked.

In Genesis 12:17 the Lord finally gets mentioned. And not because Sarai went to the altar. It says, "The Lord inflicted serious diseases on Pharaoh and his household because of Abram's wife Sarai." This is a disturbing verse. Much can be discussed, debated, or disputed. All too often followers of Jesus get stuck in the literal context of a verse and miss the application. Don't misunderstand, it is not suggested we ignore what happened; rather, the insinuation is to consider what's going on from all vantage points.

Asking *why would God do that* is the wrong question, with a misguided focus, and a narrow perspective. God is a promise keeper. God shared his promise with Sarai. God communicated his plan with Abram. He told them they would have offspring. This plan would require Sarai getting pregnant by Abram, not the Pharaoh. Their half-truth put God's plan in grave jeopardy.

These two flailing followers had lost perspective and focus. They were on a downward spiral, a slippery slope, and it lasted long enough to gain the Pharaoh's trust. They had acquired all kinds of wealth because Pharaoh gave it to them. While Abram was trusting in his own wiles, God was attempting to get their attention.

God loves His children. He loved Abram and Sarai before He called them, as He called them, and after He called them. He still passionately loves them even when they're disobeying and ignoring Him. God's plan for this couple is still His plan for this couple. Their ignorance and lack of faith didn't redirect Almighty's plan. But He needed to get their attention, to stop them from wandering and set these flailing followers back on His straight path. And he does by inflicting serious disease on the Pharaoh's household.

With Sarai in Pharaoh's court, under false pretenses, their lies spreading, she is at great risk of never coming back to Abram. They need to be caught.

KEY POINT: GETTING CAUGHT IS GOD'S PROTECTION

Genesis 12:18-19 says, "Pharaoh summoned Abram, 'what have you done...why didn't you tell me...why did you say...here is [Sarai], take her and go!"

They're caught. Caught lying, caught deceiving. Caught. And it's a good thing. Being caught is a gift from God. Caught doesn't get them into trouble, but keeps them from getting further into the trouble they created. Caught is what opens these flailing followers' eyes. Caught keeps a flailing follower from becoming a permanently failing follower. Caught sheds light on the shadows of shame cast on their hearts.

God did not forget His covenant with Sarai and her husband. They should have stayed, but instead they strayed.

Sarai stopped following God with her whole heart, and she needed to be caught. Half-hearted devotion is untrustworthy. In Genesis 12:10-13:3 the voice of God is absent because His followers stopped seeking him.

Jeremiah 29:13 says, "You will seek me and find me when you seek me with all your heart."

Abram and Sarai stopped seeking the Lord with all their heart. How do we know this? In Genesis 12:8 it's recorded that they built an altar to the Lord. In 13:4 it's written that they return to where they had been earlier - where they had first built an altar to the Lord.

Followers of Jesus must remain where they can hear his voice. Half-hearted following has a difficult time discerning God's still small voice. I recently heard a preacher say God speaks in a still small voice so we'll draw closer to him and hear him.

In between where Sarai was supposed to be (at the altar) and where she went (Egypt) is a place called the Negev, a dry wasteland. In between stayed and strayed is a wasteland.

KEY POINT: A WASTELAND DOES NOT NEED TO BE A TOTAL WASTE

God will never waste a famine in your life. A famine can be an opportunity for a wholehearted follower, even if it doesn't make sense. Being consumed with the wasteland is a waste of your time and spiritual strength. It's a struggle to follow God with your whole heart when part of it is occupied by a wasteland. The result is getting stuck on your faith journey as a halfhearted follower.

I strayed, and I was stuck. Shame was to blame because I was settled in a wasteland. Out of his great love for me, I was caught and God's grace went to work in my life. In that safe seminary community, surrounded by others who were also eager to serve Jesus with their whole hearts, God revealed this wasteland and refused for it to be a waste in my life.

When this dry place erupted in my life, it came

unscheduled and unannounced. God wasn't surprised. He actually scheduled it. This patch of wasted land in my heart needed to be inhabited by Jesus. I had tolerated the shame that had cast a shadow over this area of my heart for so long and even accommodated it. Jesus moved in and consumed the wasteland.

One morning I was in a Bible study surrounded by 100 other women. As Beth was teaching, the Holy Spirit spoke to me. I didn't hear an audible voice, rather a question was posed. "Ellen, are you willing to be broken for me?" I recognized His voice. Like any good follower of Jesus, I responded with a resounding, internal, "Absolutely, Lord!"

Days later I was a mess as God took me at my word. And what a beautiful mess it turned out to be. *You will seek me and find me when you seek me with all your heart.* He did not waste this opportunity in my life as he revealed a wasteland of hidden shame in my heart.

It wasn't an overnight transformation. It wasn't an easy road to travel. Jesus walked me through that desert to reclaim the ground where shame once hid. But here I am, over twenty years later, without the shadow of that particular shame claiming any part of my heart. God always does what he says he'll do. He reclaimed a wasted place in my heart that shame once occupied.

Genesis 13:4 says,"...they called on the name of the Lord."

Sarai and Abram left Egypt and returned to where they had first built an altar to the Lord. And they did something significant. They called on the name of the one who first called them. This word *called* has different meanings. As she was altered, Sarai *cried* out to God, she *summoned* Him to the shame, she *invited* him to fill the hidden places, and she *proclaimed* the name of the Lord. Sarai is a wholehearted follower.

As you abide at the altar, consider the name above all other names. He is Jesus. He knows your name – he desires to determine your identity and fill your heart with his joy as you call on his name. Follow Him with your whole heart.

PONDER

deeply, carefully, and thoughtfully consider

1. Consider how half-hearted following hinders a
   relationship with Jesus.

2. What needs to adjust or change in your life to
   become a wholehearted follower of Jesus?

PERSUADE
God's Word influences, encourages, and guides

1. Sarai strayed when trouble came her way. What is your common reaction or response to a crisis?

2. According to Jeremiah 29:13, when will you find God?

3. The *hand of God* protected Sarai and delivered her from the Egyptian palace. The *grace of God* allowed Abram and Sarai to leave with all they had acquired while in Egypt. How do you describe the difference between the hand of God and the grace of God?

PRACTICAL
applying Biblical Truth to present day

1. Spiritual disciplines help you to wholeheartedly follow Jesus. Using a scale of 1 – 5 [1 = rarely, 5 = regularly] rate yourself in these areas:

   a. Prayer   _____
   b. Reading your Bible   _____
   c. Bible Study   _____
   d. Church Attendance   _____
   e. Giving
       1. your time   _____
       2. your treasures   _____
       3. your talents   _____

2. What area, or areas, need your attention? What will you do about it?

PERSONAL
inviting Jesus into your current reality

1. Lives are altered at the altar. How could applying this to your life allow you to stand unashamed?

2. Name a wasteland from your life. Will you give God permission to use it so it no longer wastes anymore space in your heart?

3
Hagar
my name is victim

When our four older children were 16, 18, 20, and 21, Kevin and I adopted two more children, a brother and sister. These biological siblings were in need of a forever family. They were seven and almost six when they were born in our hearts and came into our lives. When we made the decision to adopt, we knew we wanted a sib set (biological siblings), early elementary age, and a different race than ours. We also knew we'd adopt through the foster system in our state.

The term *forever family* was new to us. I know what family is. I know what forever means. Prior to adoption I never put the two words together. They now have great significance to us Harbin's. My youngest two, Jaylen and Sukanya, had family. But horrible circumstances caused that to fall apart. Having parental rights terminated causes deep wounds and terrible suffering. Some would say my kids are victims.

Victim. The shortened definition is someone who suffers, is deceived, or cheated. My two children were born to a woman whose problems and issues became bigger than her ability to control them. They controlled her. Her turmoil and trouble became their confusion and shame. Her life choices, her havoc wrecked chaos in their hearts. The decisions she made affected them. Changes she should have made, but didn't, affected them.

People make poor choices all the time. People make mistakes. People sin. When people choose poorly, others suffer. When people lie, others are deceived. When people sin, others get cheated. My children suffered, they were deceived, and they were cheated. Some would call them victims.

I don't.

Wait.

Don't stop reading. Stay with me. I didn't say they weren't victimized. I said I don't call them victims.

Perhaps you can identify with my children. You, too, have suffered because of someone else's poor choices. Like my husband, maybe your parents divorced. Like both my mom and my dad, who were both raised with an alcoholic parent in their home. My husband and each of my parents knew a chaos I have never known. Maybe your parents moved a lot or had financial burdens. It could be one of your parents was incarcerated or perhaps, absent from your life.

Possibly through the gene pool a character trait, a health issue, a psychological problem, or an emotional propensity was passed onto you. Your grandmother was impatient, so are you. Your father was diabetic, so are you. Your mother experienced depression, so do you. Your grandpa was angry, so are you.

As a follower of Jesus these issues of suffering, deception, and being cheated continue to badger you. Following Jesus does not mean the negative people or the wake they've left behind goes away. Too many women continue to see themselves as a shamed victim. When you said yes to Jesus and He took over your life, He also took over your identity.

KEY POINT: SHAME IS NO LONGER YOUR NAME. NEITHER IS VICTIM.

Too many Christian women are living with a victim mentality, accommodating and tolerating the lie that she has no choice but to suffer from what was cheated from her life. She lives everyday as if the nametag she wears bears the name victim. Hagar is a woman who assumed this identity, bearing the name, victim. Before we go any further with her story, we need some backstory. Back to Sarai for a moment.

Genesis 16:1 says, "Now Sarai, Abram's wife, had borne him no children..."

It's now ten years since Sarai returned from Egypt. Abram is 85 years old and Sarai is 75. This verse reminds us she is still childless. Ten years later and Sarai's circumstance is the same. Ten years later and God's promise hasn't changed. God's words never fail. God's word is unchanging. Women who assume the identity of victim need to heed God's word. Hebrews 6:18 says, "It is impossible for God to lie." Those who walk by faith trust this truth.

KEY POINT: GOD WILL NOT LIE BECAUSE HE CANNOT LIE

God said he would make Abram into a great nation, and that requires a son. But Sarai is barren. Ten years earlier they walked by sight right into another king's court where she was put in his harem. They lied about Sarai being Abram's sister, and they got caught. They were kicked out of that kingdom, when in fact, according to Egypt's law, they should have been hung for their actions. God rescued his wandering, flailing followers, proving his grace to be wider and deeper than their poor choices.

Consequences come from poor choices. Consequence came to Sarai. Why would God rescue her and then punish her with consequences? Asking this question keeps you stuck with your perspective skewed.

My adopted children have consequences in their life from past choices, horrible and horrific choices of other people. Kevin and I are passionately determined that our two children receive and understand proper perspective on the horrendous circumstances of which they innocently became a part. We're resolved that the identity of victim never be written in permanent ink on their nametag. Consequences in their lives from the poor choices of other people are not God's punishment on my children. Never.

What about for the one responsible for consequence? Like Sarai, she chose poorly – leaving the safety of God's protective boundaries, going to Egypt and having her life placed in extreme danger, and lying to cover her poor choices - what about that? She'll certainly have consequences. Is that punishment?

KEY POINT: CONSEQUENCES ARE NOT PUNISHMENT, THEY'RE DISCIPLINE

Punishment is to handle severely as a penalty.

Discipline is by way of correction.

God disciplines his followers. Consequences are his correction from the result of sin. Discipline is what God does out of his great, unending love for his followers. He desires for you to learn from your mistakes. A consequence is a reminder of what your poor choice caused, helping you not to be a repeat offender.

Sarai's consequences, reminders of when she halfheartedly followed, were all around her. Reminders of how awful she was? No. Reminders of God's mean-spirited punishments? No. They were reminders of God's grace. For ten years she lived unashamed, abiding at the altar, trusting God's promise to her with these consequences not affecting her behavior or attitude but, rather, serving as reminders of God's amazing grace.

Yet, but. This little word, but, has a huge impact. This compelling conjunction does more than conjoin two thoughts. It introduces a complicated consequence.

Genesis 16:1 reveals, "Now Sarai had no children...BUT...she had an Egyptian maidservant named Hagar."

I mean no disrespect to Hagar. If I were face-to-face with these women, I would not look Hagar in the eyes and tell her she is a complicated consequence. (More on this in the next paragraph.) However, if I was with Sarai, I would refer to this Egyptian maidservant as a complicated consequence. Yes, this maidservant has a name, and no different from Sarai, she is a valuable, worthy woman to be treated with respect and dignity. Speaking truth to Sarai and referring to Hagar as a complicated consequence doesn't take away her value as a woman.

Too many women ignorantly apply mercy. It's absolutely acceptable to have mercy on Hagar. But we can't allow mercy or compassion to blind us from seeing the bigger picture. That doesn't help Hagar or Sarai. Mercy and consequence must be separated. Mercy can be fully applied in the fact that Hagar is present in Sarai's home and is a complicated consequence.

This could have been a topic of discussion between Abram and Sarai. There are a lot of situations that get avoided in our lives because we aren't willing to discuss the difficulty connected to them. If Kevin and I avoided talking with Jaylen and Sukanya about the facts of their past, how does that help them? Isn't it enough to show them all kinds of mercy? No, it's not enough. There are still obvious consequences present from someone else's choices. How does ignoring and avoiding them help my children? It doesn't. It actually harms them. And I refuse to allow hidden shame to dwell in their hearts because I wouldn't discuss the difficulties of their past.

Sarai has a maidservant. She has someone to help with the laundry, the cooking, the cleaning, and the errands, so this doesn't seem a problem. Hagar helping with the housekeeping isn't the issue.

When Abram & Sarai got booted out of Egypt, they were rich. They acquired cattle, donkeys, camels, silver, gold, menservants AND maidservants. They became wealthy. When they took matters into their own hands, they walked out of Egypt with all they had acquired.

What a blessing! Whoa. Be very careful here. Blessing comes from walking in complete obedience to God. Sarai stepped out of God's plan and made her own. This home-made plan produced a maid. None of the things Abram and Sarai acquired while in Egypt are blessings from God, rather, they are proof of God's grace. And that's a big difference.

Sarai has consequences from her disobedient trek to Egypt. Hagar is part of the consequence. Hagar is not to be held responsible for being in Sarai's home. Hagar is where she was never supposed to be. Hagar is suffering from someone else's poor choice. Hagar has been deceived and cheated. That makes Hagar a victim. Sarai is ignorant and avoids the obvious. Out of frustration, impatience, and distrust she makes another massive poor choice, and Hagar is affected.

KEY POINT: SHAME HAS YOU BLAME GOD

In Genesis 16:2, Sarai tells Abram, "the Lord has kept me from having children."

Barrenness caused deep pain for Sarai. Culturally a woman's significance was directly related to bearing children. In today's culture there are many women who experience this same pain from the same inability to conceive. If you're a woman who knows this pain personally, I am truly sorry for your heartache. Before my sympathy and prior to this particular pain settling into your life, God was aware.

God has always been aware. When a horrible hurt affects you and lands in your life, God does not get caught off-guard, surprised by any chaos. He is never found on his throne wringing his hands from worry, fretting over what to do next, asking the heavenly hosts what happened and what should happen next. God knows your pain. God is never unaware of the shame caused by your pain. For now, please allow this truth to bring peace to your troubled heart.

There are valuable insights to gain on how to handle the hidden shame allowed by someone else's pain and poor choices so you can be a woman unashamed and living as Jesus intends.

Sarai tells her husband that God kept her from having children, and this skewed perspective will keep her stuck in the shame of her unmet desire, acting out in ungodly ways. Sarai is not explaining her barrenness to her husband; rather, she is blaming God for the barrenness.

As an omniscient, all-knowing God, nothing escapes His understanding. Technically Sarai is right. God has kept her from having children. Sarai is blaming God because He hasn't delivered on His promise. She trusted God at 65, so why not now at 75? Frustration and impatience have Sarai blaming God for not delivering on his promise in her expected timeframe, causing the shadow of distrust to hide in shame in her heart.

Let the internal chaos begin. Sarai is no longer willing to wait for the promises of God. She blames God and then, continuing in Genesis 16:2, Sarai says to her husband, "Go sleep with my maidservant."

WHAT?!?! Is that really what she said? That can't be right. Everything about that sounds so wrong. Do you need to verify that passage? Go ahead – go get your Bible and look it up. Genesis 16:2. See? It's there. At the beginning of her sentence she blames God, takes a breath, and continues, *go sleep with my maidservant.*

Sometimes I read the Bible, and I wonder why women waste their time reading stupid smut novels. If you want drama, pick up the Bible. It's filled with all kinds of scandalous narratives. But there's always redemptive purpose when reading the stories God allowed in his word.

Back then it was culturally acceptable for a man to marry another woman. With his wife's full knowledge of the plan, the man could have more offspring. In Abram's case, a son could be produced. After all, inheritance was of the utmost importance. His name needed to be carried on. Another man-made plan to get what man wants.

Just because this was acceptable in man's eyes does not mean God ordained such an idea. This ancient custom was designed and determined by man to fit their culture. This brings up a good point. Where did they get that idea of having more than one wife? If you answered Egypt, then you're correct. Egypt's culture influenced theirs. Followers of God should only be influenced by him. God's ways must be done his way.

Sarai's way is wrong because it isn't God's way. In one moment she has blamed God for not doing what he said he would. (She told her husband to sleep with the maidservant.) And then she reasons it out. *Perhaps I can build a family through her.* Sarai has been deceived to believe that culture trumps covenant.

KEY POINT: GOD'S WILL MUST BE DONE GOD'S WAY

One of the biggest, most blatant, and recurring evidences that a follower of Jesus has shame in her heart is when she is focused on herself. Sarai says, *Perhaps I can.*

Years ago there was a popular bumper sticker that

annoyed me. It was a simple message. *God is my co-pilot.* Even as a young girl I was confused when I saw it proudly stuck to some bumpers of vehicles in the church parking lot. Why would they want God as their co-pilot? Like Sarai, perhaps they thought God couldn't so they can. If God's the co-pilot, then who's the pilot? Apparently Saria had one of those stickers attached to the rump of her camel. Move over, God, Sarai is now in control of your plan.

Sarai asserts herself, overriding God's ways and instituting the perhaps-I-can plan. Instead, her plan should have been *let's-go-to-the-altar-and-have-our-lives-altered.* Ignoring the altar, it's all about her and her plan now. In an attempt to be in control of her life, she will soon find herself out of control.

In Genesis 16:3-4 Sarai's plan works. Hagar gets pregnant. Yay! Now Sarai will have what she's always wanted. You see, it wasn't so bad to give God a hand. After all, He's busy taking care of the universe and paying attention to all of His other followers. He has a lot going on – prayers to hear, offerings to accept. Sarai taking matters into her own hands, and for just this once, it isn't such a big deal. Why, look, Hagar is pregnant, Abram now has a son God promised them.

Whoa. Hold up. That's not true. Abram has a son that Sarai planned, not the son God promised. Please don't call your plan God's promise. God's promise must come from God's plan. His will must be done his way.

Look at Genesis 16:4. "When Hagar knew she was pregnant, she began to despise [Sarai]"

Hagar is an Egyptian. She isn't even supposed to be in this far-away land. She should have remained in Egypt. When Sarai and her husband messed up years ago, Hagar ended up being escorted out of her hometown in a hurry. Hagar is pregnant with another woman's husband so that this other wife can raise Hagar's baby as her own child. Even though Hagar is familiar with this custom, she doesn't like it. And now Hagar despises the one who conjured up this whole plan.

Hagar is a victim here, stuck in the aftermath of someone else's sin. She is suffering and feeling cheated out of what rightfully should be hers – the child growing in her womb.

As the older, wiser, and faithful follower of God, Sarai should take the higher road and do the right thing. A woman on the perhaps-I-can plan only sees herself resulting in a pile-up of poor choices.

Genesis 16:5 records, "Then Sarai says to Abram, you are responsible for the wrong I am suffering..."

Try to imagine what Sarai looked like and how she sounded when she spoke these words. I imagine a bitter, angry, frustrated old lady, hands on her hips – ok, make that one hand on her hip because the other one is ramrod straight with her pointer finger in a staccato rhythmic pattern jutting at Abram's face with every syllable as she said, "you-are-re-spon-si-ble-for-the-wrong-I-am-suf-fer-ing!" And as every syllable was spoken her voice got higher and louder.

A pile-up of poor choices keeps piling up.

Can things get any worse? Yes. Yes, they can and they certainly do.

Sarai has heard enough from Hagar, so she does the same thing Eve did – she blames someone else instead of taking responsibility for her own poor choices, she is deceived to believe someone else is to blame. Enter shame, once again. Sarai's perhaps-I-can plan isn't working so well for anyone. You can be sure that shame from this behavior is taking up a huge space in her heart. And things only get worse.

It needs to be said that throughout all of these actions, these poor choices, the rampant sin being committed by followers of God, He is not absent. God may seem silent, but how can a woman screaming, yelling, casting blame, pointing fingers, or refusing to take responsibility hear God's voice anyway? He's waiting for her temper tantrum to calm down. When a woman is emotionally ramped up, calling the shots in her life, she has turned a deaf ear and a blind eye to God.

Sarai mistreated Hagar so Hagar leaves. (see Genesis 16:6) Hagar fled. *Leaving* implies she took time to pack a bag, rent a camel, and simply disappear. The word *fled*, means she put to flight, she ran away in a hurry. Sarai began mistreating Hagar, and Hagar was out of there. A shame-filled woman mistreats another shamed woman. What a shame!

When a follower of Holy God puts her agenda in front of God's promises, when she is guided by her emotions instead of walking by faith, forgetting that Omniscience rescued her from a previous life-altering fiasco because she abandoned his altar, then chaos will erupt in her life. Sarai's way is not God's way, and now shame is in the way of her heart.

KEY POINT: HURTING PEOPLE HURT PEOPLE

This is a true statement that has given me perspective and guided my focus when hurt has hit my life. Everyone gets hurt…unfairly, unnecessarily, inappropriately, excessively, dishonestly, unjustly, irrationally, improperly, tactlessly hurt, usually someone else who is also hurting.

Everyone has hurt someone else. Because hurting people hurt people. Since this is true, is it correct to assume the world is full of victims? This seemingly unavoidable vicious cycle turns out victims. Right?

I know people get hurt. I know this hurt can run deep. Not only have I personally experienced it, but I have seen it firsthand in my home and in my family, especially with my two youngest children. I could take a great deal of paper space to explain how the neglect and abandonment of their biological parents hurt my precious son and daughter. I can give you an array of detailed examples of what this hurt attempts to do in their lives. And every detail of their hurt would attach back to birth parents. My children are victims of their biological parents' poor choices. This is true. But. I want this conjunction to effectively portray this next thought: but my children do not need to wear victim as an identifier to whom they are.

How do I raise my daughter to follow Jesus with the shame of being a victim casting shadows on her heart? Do I raise her to wear the name victim because that's just the way it is, so she may as well figure out now how to live the rest of her life accommodating and tolerating the shame from the hurt inflicted by someone else's poor choices? If she's going to wear the name *victim*, then she will also bear that name, live it out, reflect the name, act the name, be the name.

This is completely unacceptable to me. I absolutely refuse to have my daughter wear or bear the name victim. Her identity is found only in Jesus, not in what happened to her as a young child. It's also not found in any hurt inflicted on her. And it's certainly not found in any shame stuck in her heart. Knowing you're a victim and wearing *victim* like a nametag, as an identifier of who you are, is not the same. Her identity – who she is, the name she wears, the name she bears – is found in Jesus Christ, her Savior and her Lord. Because *He* says so. She belongs to Jesus; therefore, He has all authority to determine her identity, not some hidden shame left by the hurt of someone else.

Sarai was hurting, and she hurt Hagar. Hagar is now suffering as a victim of Sarai's poor choices. Sarai cursed Hagar, she disrespected her, she thought her to be trifle and treated her with dishonor and contempt. Sarai made her maid mad, so mad that Hagar turns and runs away without a plan. Both of these women's hearts are messy. Sarai was provoked by Hagar. Hagar responded to the provocation. Hagar was the maidservant, Sarai her authority. They experienced mutual disrespect, mutual insult, and mutual disregard for the other.

Each woman is responsible for her own behavior and attitude. Each woman must own her own mess. Shame enters a heart when a woman refuses to take responsibility for her own mistakes. It also enters a heart when she assumes the responsibility of another or uses the poor choices of another as her excuse for her own sin. My daughter knows her biological mother made mistakes. Big ones. Bad ones. My daughter also knows these poor choices affect her and may continue to affect her.

My daughter has also heard, many times, that she may not use these hurts as excuses for the poor choices she may make in life. We want our precious girl to take responsibility for her poor choices, not deflect responsibility. Deflection is another way for shame to remain hidden and cause chaos in her heart.

Sarai deflected when she blamed God and Abram. Abram deflected when he put it back on Sarai. Hagar deflected when she defected.

Troubled circumstances are not permission for you to act however you feel is best. Sarai was on the perhaps-I-can-plan and now, Hagar has taken the liberty to act on that same plan by doing what she thought best by escaping her chaos.

Or so she thought. Running away, defecting from your current reality does not escape internal chaos as it goes where you go. Hagar is a victim, but she also is a part of the problem. Having a victim mentality keeps her stuck with internal chaos hiding and disrupting her life.

Hagar is hurting and she is reaping the consequences of another woman's poor choices. She's out of there. Physically, she left. Emotionally, she is done. Hagar is a victim without a plan.

KEY POINT: GOD LOVES YOU RIGHT WHERE YOU ARE, BUT HE LOVES YOU TOO MUCH TO LEAVE YOU THERE

God passionately, completely, fully, totally, and unconditionally loves Hagar. And there is nothing she can do about it. He doesn't love her because she's a victim. He loves her because he's God - it's who he is and what he does. He loves people. He loved Hagar when she was in Egypt. He loved Hagar when she was made a maidservant. He loved her when Sarai took matters into her own hands. He loved Hagar when she became Abram's second wife. He loved her when she became pregnant. God loved Hagar when she was being victimized by Sarai. God loved Hagar when she put to flight and ran away. God loved Hagar right where she was but He loved her too much to leave her there.

Genesis 16:7 proves His love for her, "The angel of the Lord found Hagar near a spring in the desert"

You can run away, but God knows where you are at all times. Hagar ran away. Her name actually means *forsaken* and *flight*. Her given name of Hagar and her assumed name of victim have stolen her identity. She has an identity crisis. God is fully aware and does something about it.

He pursued her. God went after her. The Lord found her. He did not participate in a game of hide and seek. She didn't care to be sought; she didn't have a plan. The only thing on her agenda was to flee.

God sends the angel to her. He commands the angel to go to Hagar. Did you catch that repeated word? Not just any angel, *the* angel of *the* Lord. Wow. Psalm 91:11 says, "For he will command his angels concerning you to guard you." God commanded his angel to go to Hagar. *The* angel assigned by *the* Lord was commanded to find Hagar – to go to Hagar – and to guard her.

The angel finds Hagar near a spring in the desert. A *spring*. In the *desert*.

Would you please allow that to sink in? Do not read any further until you fully grasp what God has done for Hagar. *The* angel of *the* Lord found Hagar near a spring in *the* desert. God commanded an angel to find Hagar smack dab in the middle of her desert experience. This hurting victim is pursued by holy God. (I can't even write this without tears spilling from my eyes.)

And God is not silent. Imagine Hagar on the run with her victim mindset, her hurting heart, her broken dreams, pregnant, in the driest place of her life and out of nowhere someone starts speaking to her. As we read the story we understand that it's the angel of the Lord is who speaking to her. But she has no clue who the angel is. The first word out of the angel's mouth must have stopped her in her tracks. "Hagar," the angel calls her by her name.

This is significant. The Lord knows her name. In the Bible when one angel is recorded as speaking, the angel is God's mouthpiece. Any word out of an angel's mouth has been approved and authorized by God himself. Hagar is confronted in her desert experience by someone who knows her name. I love that God calls her Hagar. He didn't call her Miss Victim or Miss

Shame. No, he called her by name. Because God loves her, he calls her. Because he loves her, he knows her.

Years ago, on a Sunday morning in church, we were singing a song with the phrase *he knows my name*. Behind me was a young boy about six years old. As we repeated the phrase *he knows my name*, this little guy turned to his momma and with an unexpected excitement exclaimed, "he really *does* know my name." I will never forget the look on that boy's face when he realized this truth.

My friend and mentor, Beth, loves Jesus very much. She is an example to me of how to wholeheartedly and unashamedly follow Jesus. When Beth and I pray over the phone, often she'll begin with this "Jesus, it's Beth and Ellen."

It had never occurred to me to introduce myself as I begin to pray. I've pondered Beth's announcement as she connects with God. I love that she confidently approaches the throne of grace. I'm awed by the intimacy she has with her Lord. Unashamed followers of Jesus can approach him with confidence, trusting his love and comprehending that he fully knows them. Beth doesn't introduce herself because God doesn't know her, she introduces herself because of the intimacy she has with Jesus.

Perhaps you're similar to Hagar. Someone else's sin has allowed shame on your heart, and you're wearing and possibly bearing the name *victim*. Jesus desires to approach you the same way the angel approached Hagar. Hebrews 13:8 says, "Jesus Christ is the same yesterday and today and forever." He doesn't change.

You are loved by an unchangeable God. Hebrews 6:17-19 says, "God wanted to make the unchanging nature of his purpose very clear…by two unchangeable things in which it is impossible for God to lie, we who have **FLED** to take hold of the hope offered to us may be greatly encouraged. We have this hope as an anchor for the soul, firm and secure."

Miss Victim or Mrs. Shame, you have fled because of deep hurt, but it's time to shed these nametags, this identity. You are loved, and your heart is safe with a truth-telling, hope-filled, immovable anchor named Jesus. When you are saved by his grace, when you said yes to Jesus, He began sharing His name with you. You belong to Him. He is your identity. Take hold of the hope named Jesus, who is your soul's anchor. In Him your identity is firm and secure.

After we adopted Jaylen and Sukanya, Kevin suggested we have a birth certificate celebration. Jaylen and Sukanya were permanently moved into our family for seven months before the judge ruled their adoption final at the official court hearing. It took another few months for their official birth certificates to arrive with their parents officially named Kevin and Ellen Harbin along with their names forever changed to Harbin.

Our four older kids were geographically scattered, making gathering as a family a challenge. One weekend, soon after the birth certificates arrived, all eight Harbins were home. We scheduled that birth certificate party. After dinner, we gathered in our living room. Kevin had eight birth certificates in his hands. He handed them out to each rightful owner.

Beginning with the eldest Harbin, that's Kevin, and descending in birth order, we each read our names, our place of birth, and our parents' names as sited on each personalized certificate. I clearly remember each of my six children individually proclaiming their name to be "_____

_____ Harbin". When Jaylen and Sukanya said their names out loud, we all listened with rapt attention. Whatever their last names were before they were adopted had been removed from their identity.

When the angel spoke Hagar's name, God was reminding Hagar who she was. He was rewriting her nametag. It's like God said, "Hagar, though you were victimized, I do not see a victim. I see Hagar, the woman I love." God wants to get Hagar's attention. He loves her too much to leave her in her victim mindset.

Not only does God get her attention by calling her by name, he also reminds her where she belongs. He says, "Hagar, servant of Sarai..." I love his gentleness. Like a velvet hammer God gently, but firmly, reshapes her mindset and sets her straight. She fled, so truth must be shed, or she'll continue to be deceived that she's a victim. She was victimized, that's true, but it no longer identifies her. God reclaimed that.

Where have you come from?

Where are you going?

These are two questions, from an angel, delivered to one woman, by one loving God. Omniscience asking questions. Irony. He asks for Hagar's sake. God is loving Hagar too much to leave her stuck in the desert, as a victim.

She answers. Genesis 16:8 continues, "…I'm running away from my mistress Sarai." She knows exactly where she comes from (her mistress, Sarai), but she doesn't have a plan of where she's going (I'm running away.) The angel of the Lord pulls out the velvet hammer again. Gently, but firmly, God corrects and sets her straight.

In Genesis 16:9 God told her to go back to her mistress and submit to her. The key word here is *told*. This is not a suggestion; God is not giving her an option, but straight up told her what to do. If you're thinking *that's not right for him to demand that she go back and be victimized*; then you need correcting as well.

God is not telling her to go back and be a victim. He reminded her who she is, and now he is making her aware of his plan for her life. So far, Sarai made a plan for Hagar's life. God, not Sarai, is now in charge of Hagar. He needs Hagar to return for his plan to be set in motion, for her and her child. Remember, she's pregnant with Abram's child. Hagar needs to return because God desires to bless this woman, and obedience is what brings the blessing.

Before the angel of the Lord leaves Hagar's side, God has more to say. Recorded in Genesis 16:10-12, [10] "The angel added, 'I will so increase your descendants that they will be too numerous to count.' [11] The angel of the Lord also said to her: 'You are now with child and you will have a son. You shall name him Ishmael, for the Lord has heard your misery. [12] He will be a wild donkey of a man; his hand will be against everyone and everyone's hand against him, and he will live in hostility toward all his brothers."

Well, there you have it, encouraging words from *the* angel of *the* Lord.

She will give birth to a son. His descendants will be too numerous to count. God has been listening to her, and he's fully aware of her misery. After the encouraging words were spoken, God was honest with her as he laid out what her future looked like. Blessing and consequence are interwoven in this message delivered to Hagar through God's angel. Her son will be a wild donkey of a man, a fighter. He will fight and be fought. Hostility will be present against his brothers.

Wild has a new meaning since I've raised boys. I had no idea what to expect when the doctor announced *it's a boy*. I'm glad I didn't know ahead of time what kind of things were in my future. I'm not sure how I would have responded had someone told me my boys would love to play sting-pong, which is removing their shirts and seeing how hard they could serve a ping pong at each other's bare bellies and then proudly displaying the red marks produced by the sting of the ping pong ball as it hit their exposed skin. Wild.

Raising my boys, and still raising another, to become men was rough at times. We had tough days, difficult times. I've heard 'he's so, ummm...active' or 'wow, he sure has a lot of energy.' Wild. And I love it. Taming active behavior is a challenge for the mom raising wild boys. Those wild boys can become men who passionately follow Jesus – I do not desire to tame that!

Hagar had a slight idea what she was facing as she prepared for her son's birth. She knew her son would be a wild donkey. Research has taught me that this wasn't terrible news. Donkeys are cautious, stubborn, and observant. They have keen hearing and a good sense of vision and smell. They're social creatures, interacting with other animals. Donkeys aggressively protect their own, willing to attack whatever is a threat to them or their young. That's not bad news for Hagar. We, though, hear *wild* and jump to assumptions, even conclusions.

It would make more sense for us to get riled over Hagar

having to return to a mean, spiteful, nasty, unkind, cruel old lady – who by the way, is your husband's first childless wife. Oh – and your boss. That is a wild to avoid.

But God said go back.

After Hagar hears what the angel of the Lord has to say, she has a response.

KEY POINT: ANY ENCOUNTER WITH GOD COMPELS A RESPONSE

Ignoring God can be a response to his word. Avoiding God can be a response to his word. Apathy can be a response to God's word. Half-hearted listening can be a response to his word. God desires openness and a complete trust when responding to his word.

Hagar responds in Genesis 16:13, "You are the God who sees me...I have now seen the One who sees me."

Incredible. Extraordinary. An absolutely beautiful response to God's word. Moments earlier this woman was tolerating and accommodating hidden shame in her heart. She was wearing and bearing the identity of a victim. Now she is calling on the name of the One who sees her, Jehovah. And she is exclaiming that God, the mighty one, is who she now sees.

How did Hagar recognize God? How did she know who he was? Hagar lived with Sarai for ten years. The past few months do not define who Sarai truly is. Ten years earlier when Sarai and Abram left Egypt, Hagar was present as they returned to where they had first built an altar to the Lord. Hagar witnessed the re-altering in Sarai's life as she dwelled at the altar. God was not ignored or avoided by Sarai for ten years. Sarai became frustrated with God and acted out of that desperation. She was wrong, but she was still a follower of God. She was a misguided follower who made horrible choices, and those choices affected Hagar. (More on Sarai in the next chapter.)

As Hagar responded to God's voice in her persecuted place, she fixed her eyes on him and gained proper perspective. Prior to her encounter with God, she was caught in the shame of what was done to her, how she was victimized, and what happened because of someone else's poor choices. With a victim mind-set she tried to function, but this only made room in her heart for shadows of hidden shame to take up residence and bring chaos. Accommodating and tolerating shame messed with her identity and brought confusion. When God showed up in her desert experience, she had eyes for her Savior, the mighty One who loved her, knew her, and called her by name. Her identity was found in him and him alone.

PONDER

deeply, carefully, and thoughtfully consider

1. Carefully consider and write down the difference between being a victim and being victimized.

2. *Hurting people hurt people.* Consider how this has affected you...
   a. when you're the one being hurt

   b. when you're the one inflicting hurt

PERSUADE

God's Word influences, encourages, and guides

1. In Genesis 16:7 the Lord found Hagar. How are you encouraged by this?

2. Read Proverbs 15:3. Hagar was mistreated, she was victimized. How could a modern-day Hagar be encouraged by this verse?

3. How can Hebrews 13:8 influence you from past hurt and harm affecting your life today?

PRACTICAL
applying Biblical Truth to present day

1. The Lord provided a spring for Hagar in the middle of her desert experience. How has He provided for you when you've been victimized?

2. Hebrews 6:18 says, "It is impossible to God to lie." How have you been deceived due to being mistreated, hurt, or wronged?

PERSONAL
inviting Jesus into your current reality

1. What consequences have you assumed were punishment rather than discipline?

2. If you've been victimized, trust Jesus with the hurt. He loves you right where you are, but too much to leave you there. The Lord reshaped Hagar's mindset, reminding her who she is and encouraging her to walk in obedience to Him. What needs to be set straight in you due to deep hurt misguiding you?

4
Sarah

my name is doubt

I doubt it. This phrase is a sure way for the Deceiver to do damage in the hidden places of your heart. The third word of this short phrase is multifaceted. It.

A two-letter word with a powerful punch. What is *it* you doubt? *I doubt he'll ever change. I doubt I can succeed. I doubt we'll have enough. I doubt he'll come. I doubt it'll fit. I doubt he'll notice. I doubt we'll see that happen. I doubt they'll be on time. I doubt she heard you. I doubt she'll forgive. I doubt the bitterness will end. I doubt I will stop worrying. I doubt he'll change. I doubt I'll know peace. I doubt joy will come. I doubt hope exists. I doubt he loves me. I doubt I'm a good mom. I doubt. I doubt* **IT**.

What's your **IT**? What do you doubt? Facing doubt is necessary to living unashamed. The dance of doubt two-steps on your heart. Deceiving and destroying - deceiving you to believe doubt must be accommodated and tolerated, destroying truth. If in a contest, this dance would be rewarded for accomplishing its goal. It's time to change who leads the dance.

Is anything too hard for the Lord? Stop. Really. Stop. Before you read on, answer the question. Is anything too hard for the Lord? Your answer matters. *Yes, maybe, I'm not sure, I'll let you know* later all mean you're in a dance of doubt.

I was swirling, twirling in the dance. As a mom, I faltered. After I took my daughter to school, I returned home to put the finishing touches on this chapter. Grabbing my mug of coffee, I sat in front of my laptop and began reading aloud. I read the first three words and let out a disgusted breath. Obviously, the Deceiver was leading. *I doubt my mothering was effective this morning.*

I kept reading. What do you doubt? *All good here, let's move on.* Continuing, is anything too hard for the Lord? *Stop, Ellen, and answer the question.* Ignoring the directive, I continued reading aloud when I was interrupted by an incoming text. Grabbing my phone, I read the text.

Thinking about you, praying for you today, friend [insert heart emoji]

I stopped, exhaled, and answered the question. *No, Lord, nothing is too hard for you. Not my stubbornness, not my impatience, nor my short-temper I blasted on my daughter this morning. The doubt I struggle with parenting this beautiful girl you chose for me to mother – even that is not too hard for You.*

The text was from a friend I met three months back at a conference. We spent five days together, long enough for a friendship to take root. She walked in the room, and immediately I knew I would like Jeanne. Extroverts tend to connect quickly in a new setting. This writer's conference was an intensive, only twelve people plus the leader. Friendships were built from the intimacy of this small group, furthering opportunity for growth.

Is anything too hard for the Lord? No! Jesus knew I was in a dance of doubt. With my gaze off Him, He needed to redirect my focus. As only the Holy Spirit can, He called on Jeanne in Missouri to pray for her friend in Michigan. Jeanne had no idea I was being led in a dance of doubt. Jeanne was clueless I was struggling to reread this manuscript. Jeanne wasn't aware I had faltered in parenting my daughter this morning. But Jesus knew. And He took back the lead.

I don't know much about dancing, and I'm not good at it. However, I love being held by my husband in a slow dance. Taking the lead, Kevin confidently guides as we glide, dancing together. What happens when I take the lead away from Kevin? Faltering. Confusion. Missteps. An effective dance requires a dependable leader.

When Jesus owns your heart, He should also operate it. Jesus dwells where Satan desires to dance. The Deceiver deludes a follower of Jesus, desiring to lead her in a dance of doubt. He takes the lead, and she missteps and falters, confused. Answering anything but no to the question *is anything too hard for the Lord* causes doubt to get accommodated and tolerated, determining identity, and stealing joy. Shame takes up residence.

If you delay taking God at His word, doubt threatens to dance. Doubt quickly turns to shame. Shame is difficult to detach from the dance floor of your soul. For a woman struggling to live as Jesus intends, Mr. D-Evil loves nothing more than to keep you stuck and confused, pulling your dance card and taking the lead.

In chapter two, Satan distracted Sarai to believe that she needed to stray from a famine. Faltering, the dance began. Hesitating to take God at His word, confused, the dance continued. Years later, doubt resurfaced when the promised son hadn't been born in her expected timeframe. Doubt took up residence from this misstep and danced on the floor of her heart.

Sarai could have avoided the dance, had she not doubted God - had she taken God at His word. Easier said than done. Sarai is no different than you or me. We have all doubted when it comes to taking God at His word. But that's an explanation of how the dance begins. Explanation does not justify participation.

Shame lands and settles in a woman's heart when she doubts God, when she hesitates to believe what he says he will do. Like a guest who overstays his/her welcome, doubt gets accommodated once the dance begins. *Will it ever leave? I doubt it.*

Sarai was 76 years old when Hagar gave birth to Ishmael. At 76 years of age, Sarai doubted God's word; she hesitated to believe what God said would happen, would happen.

Imagine, a 76-year-old woman doubting that she would become pregnant. What's wrong with her, anyway? The nerve! I can't even begin to think about my 75-year-old mom being pregnant. Ludicrous. Absurd. Preposterous. Laughable, especially to her.

At 76 years of age, a woman's ability to conceive a child has been shut down for years. Sarai's womb was no longer a candidate for conception. Her periods were long gone. Her uterus was no longer accepting eggs. Like the Negev, she assumed her womb was a wasteland. What 76-year-old woman believes she still has a chance to conceive?

KEY POINT: IS ANYTHING TOO HARD FOR THE LORD?

Sarai needed to answer this question.

Fast forward thirteen years to Genesis 17:1 where it begins, "When Abram was ninety-nine years old, the Lord appeared to him and said..."

Being ten years younger than Abram, Sarai is now 89. She still hasn't conceived the promised son. Sarai doubted God at 65 and she hesitated to believe him at 75. At 89, can you blame a lady for doubting? Whoa. Careful. Wrong question. Focusing on human emotion keeps you from recollecting God's word. Giving Sarai a pass - *give her a break, after all, she's 89 years old* – is a misstep and an opportunity for the dance of doubt to get transferred to your heart.

Doubt is an invitation for shame to get accommodated when we hesitate to answer the question. Sarai unknowingly allowed the seed of doubt, and then shame threatened to move in. Shame does not always appear the same – that's a huge part of Satan's deception. When Sarai hesitated to believe God and take him at his word, shame showed up. She lied, took matters into her own hands, and shame threatened to take up residence in her heart disguised as a little doubt.

In Genesis 12, God spoke. He told Abram he would have a son through Sarai. *Is anything too hard for the Lord?* Twenty-four years later, has God forgotten His promise? *Is anything too hard for the Lord?* God keeps His word.

Every December 25th we believe and celebrate Jesus' birth. The Virgin birth. We don't hesitate to believe. A man spent three days in the belly of a big fish. We tell the story, as if we were present, of a teenaged boy who took down a giant with one smooth stone. Jesus turned water into wine – you believe that, right? You've read about how he made a boy's happy meal feed 5000 people. Jesus made blind men see, lame men walk, a dead girl breathe, and a friend walk on water. At Easter, you stand and proclaim Jesus rose from the dead. We believe it. We don't doubt any of it.

Then why are we so quick and apt to give Sarai a pass when it comes to her doubt? *Can you blame a 65-year-old, let alone a 75-year-old, for doubting she'd get pregnant and produce the promised son?* Sarai's **IT** was huge. *I doubt it* caused the Deceiver to dance in her soul, shame to move in. Had Sarai answered, 'absolutely nothing' to the question, and believed it, there would be no room in her heart for doubt.

The year before we adopted, I was diagnosed with a rare and extremely aggressive form of uterine cancer. My gynecologic oncologist scheduled a complete hysterectomy, removing all reproductive organs, some lymph nodes, and pelvic fluids.

Kevin and I were convinced God had assigned the adoption option to our family. My cancer diagnosis caused us to question this option and threatened doubt. Did we hear wrong? Surgery was followed by chemotherapy and radiation. From diagnosis to the last round of radiation, I refused to allow doubt any space in my heart. There was no room for doubt when the doctor declared *you have cancer*.

A follower of Jesus must be resolved how she'll handle doubt when it desires to dance. The same God who called Kevin and me to adopt children also knew a cancer crisis would erupt in my life. *Is anything too hard for the Lord?* His plan of promise for our family was not disrupted, but rather, interrupted. Would I doubt or would I take God at his word? How I respond has everything to do with shame dancing on my heart. *Is anything too hard for the Lord?*

The space of time between the end of Genesis 16 and the beginning of Genesis 17 is thirteen years. It's unclear how Sarai spent these years. Was she threatened by doubt? It's been 24 years since God promised Sarai a son. Was there room for *I doubt it* in her heart?

One year separated my cancer diagnosis from our first face-to-face meeting with Jaylen and Sukanya. A year of questions. A year where doubt threatened. And yet, one thing precipitated every question, gave clarity over potential confusion, and shined brighter than doubt. Promise protected any shadow of shame from hiding in my heart.

KEY POINT: GOD IS A PROMISE KEEPER

Your questions cannot send God into a quandary. His commitment is not altered by your confusion. God is not directed by doubt. As a promise keeper, God keeps his word. Before cancer erupted in my life, I was convinced of God's promise regarding adoption. And yet, we had questions. This interrupting piece had us puzzled. Doubt surfaced. I was at a crossroads. Answering the question *is anything too hard for the Lord* was crucial as doubt threatened to dance on my soul.

Followers of Jesus need to be careful they're not carried away by doubt. A cancer diagnosis is not an excuse for the dance of doubt to direct a heart. Rather, this interruption is an opportunity to answer the question.

Though thirteen years of Sarai's life are unknown, what we know about God isn't. He is a promise keeper, and He promised Sarai a son. She is now 89-years-old and doubts God will keep his word. Doubt will dance in her heart, shame will get accommodated, her identity will get confused, and she'll be stuck on her faith journey.

Three significant conversations guide and clarify what precipitates the doubt threatening shame in Sarai's heart.

- A conversation of covenant.
- A conversation of conversion.
- A conversation of clarity.

A conversation of covenant takes place in Genesis 17:1-2. God is speaking to Abram, "I will confirm my covenant between me and you." The promise keeper confirms, establishes, and sets firm the promise.

This conversation begins (Genesis 17:1) with the Lord appearing to Abram saying, "I am God Almighty; walk before me and be blameless." El-Shaddai is speaking. We read *God Almighty* and we think, God. We read *Lord*, and we still see God. The Hebrew language, used here in its original text, has different names for God that directly connect to his character. El-Shaddai. Oh, how I love this! Translated, it means *the one to whom nothing is impossible.*

Do not misstep and miss the connection. The one to whom nothing is impossible has just begun a conversation of covenant with a 99-year-old man saying, I am the one to whom nothing is impossible – the same man who 24 years earlier was promised a son. He is the same God who called Kevin and me to adopt and the same God who wasn't defeated by a cancer diagnosis.

God established his covenant with Abram and Sarai and now, 24 years later, the one to whom nothing is impossible confronts a 99-year-old man confirming that he would indeed be the father of many nations (17:4), he would become fruitful (17:6), and the land promised to him would one day belong to his descendants (17:8). All of this could only come from one to whom nothing is impossible.

A conversation of conversion is found in Genesis 17:5. God told Abram he would now be called Abraham. A spiritual change is confirmed by a name change. In 17:15, God says, "...as for Sarai your wife, you are no longer to call her Sarai; her name will be Sarah." The one to whom nothing is impossible changes Sarai's name as a sign that she will see the promise.

God desires that Sarah, meaning princess, see herself as God sees her. The one to whom nothing is impossible says she will no longer have her identity determined by what she hasn't been able to accomplish, but rather, her identity by what God calls her – a Princess.

My sweet mom's identity was determined as a young girl by her biological father who drank, yelled, and mistreated his wife and children. He told her she couldn't do anything right, that she wouldn't amount to much. Those damaging words danced on her soul, leaving shame on her young heart.

Doubt that she could do right or be good was set in her heart, doubt she was special, doubt she was talented, doubt she was loved, doubt she mattered. The dance of doubt did the two-step in my mom – deceiving her to believe lies and potentially destroying truth regarding her identity. The one to whom nothing is impossible never took his eyes off my mom. Jesus loved her so much he couldn't take his eyes off her.

My mom's parents eventually divorced. Though her father was physically distant, the hurtful words remained intact - residing in her heart with shame casting its shadow.

A few years later, when my mom was about fifteen, my grandma began dating a man. He was a single man, who had never married and had no children. My grandma had five children; the oldest was married with her own children, the youngest was four when this man was introduced. He loved my grandma, wanted to marry her, and desired to be a father-figure to her children.

The day arrived when my mom would meet this man. When Bob met the shy, cautious girl I call mom, my grandma said, "Bob, this is my daughter, Linda." Bob responded, "It's nice to meet you, Princess."

The dance of doubt was halted; an identity conversion began. For over 50 years, Bob called my mom Princess until he took his last breath on December 31, 2010.

KEY POINT: IDENTITY IS DETERMINED BY GOD

Sarah is given a new name and has an identity conversion. The one to whom nothing is impossible has spoken. Kings of peoples will come from her. Once known as a barren woman, she's now the mother of nations. The same God who changed her name claimed her identity. Sarah's identity shouldn't be in what she hasn't been able to accomplish, but rather in what God calls her.

A conversation of clarity occurs in Genesis 17:19 when the one to whom nothing is impossible told Abraham, "Your wife Sarah will bear you a son." Twenty-four years have passed since

God called Abraham into a special relationship. It's been 24 years since they left their home and began walking in obedience to God's ways. It's been 24 years since they began walking by faith and not by sight...24 years since this woman was promised she would bear a son.

Before we go any further we must take a few steps back to 17:1. At the beginning of the conversation of covenant, immediately after El-Shaddai is introduced, God says to Abram and Sarai, "...walk before me and be blameless."

"Walk before me," God says. The word *me* translates to face. God is saying, "Sarai, wherever you go, wherever you are, wherever you land, keep my face in your vision. Follow me close to sense my presence, follow near to hear my voice, close enough to catch when I whisper."

One of my favorite valedictions, a closing remark to a note or message, is *tucked in tight*. I'm not sure where I heard it, but its meaning is deep. Imagine a small child getting tucked into her snugly covers. She's comforted and secured, firmly fixed in her safe place.

That's how El-Shaddai directs and mandates His followers to live – tucked in tight to the one to whom nothing is impossible. And then He adds *be blameless*. The King James Version says, "be thou perfect."

Did you just exhale, grunt, or do a mini Darth Vader? You read perfect and thrust your arms up, defeated. A follower who tucks in tight to Jesus stays the course, remaining firmly fixed, regardless of the directive or command.

Perfect in Genesis 17:1 means complete, to improve, or faultless. Blameless is faultless, not sinless. Blameless is whole, unimpaired, having integrity.

Sarai was charged to tuck in tight and be whole. Doubt is not tucked in tight. Doubt has holes.

These stupid warts continue to irritate me. I'm aggravated, exasperated, annoyed, and frustrated. I've been to the dermatologist every two weeks for over a year. And I still have warts. At times, I've doubted whether they'll go away. This may seem like a small doubt. Surely there's bigger, more significant issues in my life that could cause a more sympathetic doubt, right?

Ironically, when I had a high risk, aggressive cancer rampaging my body, I never doubted God's sovereignty. Not one single doubt. But pesky, ugly bumps on my digits and doubt threatens to run amuck.

KEY POINT: DOUBT LEFT UNCHECKED CAN HAVE YOU OUT OF CONTROL

Every two weeks as I'm prepping for the inevitable dermatology visit, a conversation of clarity is necessary. I know as the physician's assistant enters the room, she'll inquire, "So, how are they?" This incessant question has the potential to throw me emotionally out of control. If left unchecked, shame moves in.

The one to whom nothing is impossible is fully aware of the warts that have taken up residence on my fingers. Doubt leaves me doubting this fact. Doubt has associates — they're called hesitation, skepticism, querying, distrust. And they accompany doubt.

After God renames her Sarah, in Genesis 17:16, He tells Abraham, "I will bless her and will surely give you a son by her."

This 99-year-old man did not say, "Sarah, go prepare the nursery! The promised baby boy is coming soon!" Instead, Abraham does four things, all associated and rooted in doubt.

- Fell on his face ……………hesitation.
- Laughed to himself………..skepticism.
- Quietly questioned God……querying.
- Loudly spoke at God……….distrust.

Abraham fell facedown. Doubt directed his gaze away from God's face. A hesitation to believe God's words caused a physical reaction. Wait. Hold on a minute. This wasn't the first-time Abraham fell facedown. In 17:3, he reacted the same way - during the conversation of covenant.

Ah! Yes, he did. Though the word for facedown is the same, what motivated the reaction is different. In 17:3, though Abram fell facedown, his gaze was firmly fixed on God and His word. As Abram fell, God still had his attention. In 17:17, when Abraham fell, he was firmly fixed on himself.

The verse says Abraham laughed and spoke to himself. Have you ever laughed a bogus chuckle? Not too long ago as I disciplined my son, I fake laughed. I don't recall the infraction, but I do remember his reaction to my simulated snicker.

"Momma, why are you laughing when you're frustrated?" *Well son,* I thought, *that's because I doubt you even understand the reason for my frustration and why I'm disciplining you.* He's an adolescent. He's still growing up and has much to learn. Apparently, I do too. My skepticism as I disciplined my son caused an immature reaction that didn't help the situation.

Abraham's skeptical laugh was rooted in doubt. Skepticism birthed unspoken questions of doubt. This internal querying was heard loud and clear by God. *Will a son be born to a man 100 years old? Will Sarah bear a child at the age of 90?* Yes, the news is unbelievable, preposterous, outrageous, even laughable. But keep in mind who's speaking. It is El-Shaddai - *the one to whom nothing is impossible.*

Abraham breaks his silent querying with the audible probe, *if only.* If introduces distrust. *If only* is another way to say, *are you sure?* Doubt keeps going to deeper places inside Abraham's heart. Left unchecked emotional, mental, and spiritual life can run amuck.

God breaks through doubt. In 17:19-21 He gets Abraham's attention with another conversation. "Yes, your wife Sarah will bear you a son...by this time next year."

How does Sarah respond to this? Before that's answered, notice God has just responded to any obvious questions she may have. He has clearly communicated the who, the what, the when. She *will* be pregnant, she *will* deliver a boy, and it *will* happen within the year. He even insinuated the how - pregnant only happens one way. Sarah's response? *I doubt it.*

"So Sarah laughed to herself as she thought, 'after I am worn out and my master is old, will I now have this pleasure?" [Genesis 18:12]

Reaction is more accurate. Sarah doesn't respond – she reacts.

KEY POINT: BEFORE YOU'RE SURPRISED, STUNNED, OR SHOCKED, KNOW THE ANSWER TO THE QUESTION *IS ANYTHING TOO HARD FOR THE LORD?*

Sarah hasn't answered the question, so she reacts to the news by querying the one to whom nothing is impossible. And she's snarky about it. Doubt ignites sparks of snark.

Do I want to admit snarky has been lit in me? Of course not, but it's true. Regrettably, my snarky-ness might have won me an academy award a time or two. Dictionary.com defines snarky as testy, irritable, or having a rudely critical tone.

My heart is filled with snarky messages that ignite when doubt is present. *You've got to be kidding me! Whatever! Seriously?! I'll believe it when I see it. What took so long? Ha, that'll never happen. I'm on my last nerve with her. Don't be so dumb!*

Sadly, that's only a few examples of my snarky comebacks. Give me a good reason, and I can spark a snark faster than you can light a match. Damage and potential destruction occurs from one tiny snark. Explosions have come from my reaction to doubt sparked in my heart. Like Sarah, I've laughed to myself on many occasions when confronted with a revelation from God. Faithfully following Jesus requires having your gaze firmly on His face. When our gaze grazes in the direction of doubt, we become faltering followers.

Sarah laughed. She faltered. Instead of remaining firmly fixed on God's promise, doubt swung her focus to the who, the what, the when, and the how. This laugh is a mocking laugh, a laugh in jest. Pregnant at 89. Hard to believe? Absolutely. Impossible? Absolutely not.

Years ago, I learned a song turned saying. Or was it a saying turned song?

God said it, and I believe it
and that settles it for me

Though some may doubt that His word is true
I've chosen to believe it, now how about you?
God said it, and I believe it
And that settles it for me

We may not sing the tune today, but the words ring true. *Though some may doubt His word is true*...oh, how I pray I live out the phrase that follows...*I've chosen to believe it.*

Taking God at His word is a choice, and it requires complete faith. Otherwise, doubt steps in and starts dancing on your heart. And then you end up laughing in jest at God when He reveals the unbelievable, preposterous, and outrageous.

God confronted Sarah's doubt. In Genesis 18:13-14 God asks Abraham straight up, "Why did Sarah mock me?" implying, 'why did she doubt my word?' God confronts because He doesn't want doubt to take root inside Sarah's heart. Rooted doubt is like a weed that rapidly spreads and takes over.

God's word can stop doubt from badgering you and burrowing in your heart, determining identity and stealing joy. *Is anything too hard for the Lord* was Abraham and Sarah's confrontation. Again, the question must be answered; otherwise, if in a dance of doubt, you'll react instead of responding. Roots have Sarah entangled so she reacts, leaving fear in charge and giving birth to a lie.

Sarah saw derailment when God only delayed His promise. Sarah neglected to answer the question and became afraid, "I did not mock God," she lied. In jeopardy of further root entanglement, God has the last word in this exchange - *yes, you did laugh.* God does not want Sarah believing a lie. The one to whom nothing is impossible intends His promise be fulfilled. Sarah's doubt must be stopped.

KEY POINT: DOUBT CANNOT DERAIL GOD'S PROMISE

His plan will happen. His promise will be fulfilled. At the exact time God had promised, His will was done. Genesis 21:1-2 says, *Now the Lord was gracious to Sarah...and did for her what He had promised. Sarah became pregnant and bore a son...at the very time God had promised.*

Sarah's doubt didn't derail God's promise. A baby boy is born twenty-five years after God delivered the promise. Is anything too hard for the Lord? Do you doubt it?

There it is again, the multifaceted two-letter word. Consider what IT is that has you participating in a dance of doubt. God's word promises much. He'll supply all your needs. Jesus is the Prince of Peace. The joy of the Lord is your strength. His steadfast love never ceases. You don't need to be anxious. You are never alone. The Holy Spirit is the comforter. The Lord is your shelter in the storm. He is your rock, refuge, fortress, strong tower, ever-present help. Jesus guides, protects, heals, forgives. He knows all, and He is your all-in-all. Do you doubt **IT**?

The 'T' stands so tall, representing the promise of the cross. Jesus hung on the cross to cross out your doubt. He died on the cross and took your shame. God's word promises it. 1Peter 2:24 [New Century Version] says, "Christ carried our sins in his body on the cross so we would stop living for sin and start living for what is right. And you are healed because of his wounds."

We've been deceived to believe that shame must be accommodated and tolerated. Peter says, "Pshaw!" Jesus carried your shame. IT was nailed to the cross. Stop living with IT. Stop accommodating IT. Stop tolerating IT. When our eyes are focused on El-Shaddai, we see the one to whom nothing is impossible. He made the cross possible. He promised He would send His Son, and He would save people from their sins. He did what He promised; He did IT.

When the Deceiver has you in the dance of doubt, you're no longer focused on the cross. What blocks your view of the cross? Sometimes it's I – you, your doubt, your shame seems bigger than the cross. When **I** steps in the way, you have an obstructed view of the †.

I†

If you're in a dance of doubt, gaze on the cross. Fix your eyes on Jesus. Focus on the one to whom nothing is impossible. There is room at the cross for you - your sin, your doubt, your shame. Don't doubt it. The one to whom nothing is impossible promises it.

Is anything too hard for the Lord?

PONDER
deeply, carefully, and thoughtfully consider

1. Look deep and name what causes you doubt. How does this affect your walk with Jesus?

2. Honestly write your thoughts as you carefully consider *is anything too hard for the Lord.*

PERSUADE
God's Word influences, encourages, and guides

1. Read Matthew 14:25-31. Jesus asks Peter a question, *why did you doubt*. What did Jesus say before he asked the question? In what ways are you similar to Peter?

2. How does James 1:6 compare a doubter? How does this keep you from standing firm?

3. 1Peter 2:24 plainly says healing comes from Jesus' wounds. Do you doubt it?

PRACTICAL
applying Biblical Truth to present day

1. What hard thing is plaguing you right now? What Biblical truth needs your attention? What promise of God can you claim and apply?

2. In Genesis 17, Abraham hesitated, was skeptical, questioned God, and showed distrust when faced with doubt. How could Abraham have applied what God told him from Genesis chapter 12? [hint: *I will*]

PERSONAL

inviting Jesus into your current reality

1. Describe a time when you hesitated, showed skepticism, questioned, or distrusted God due to doubt.

2. Have you reacted surprised, stunned, or shocked to something causing doubt to take up residence in your heart? Could responding well have made a difference? How?

5
Rebekah
my name is stressed

There were about 75 women in the room. They came with expectations - most do when attending a one-day conference designed to encourage and equip them to a deeper walk with Jesus. Scattered on the tables were multicolored post-it notes. Women began jotting down the giant issues, the things blocking, hindering, obstructing them from trusting God wholeheartedly.

It was like many Davids facing their personal giants. Perched on top of a table at the front of the room was a large, throne-like chair. The table represented a woman's heart. The throne, the very place where Jesus abides, dwells, and inhabits. The invitation came to bring their giants – the tiny squares of sticky paper – and attach them to the throne of grace.

A few days after that conference, I retrieved the sticky notes from my bag. Prior to the day, I hadn't planned on reading them. But as I was processing the event, I was compelled to know what issues keep women stuck and held back on their faith journey. It took some time to categorize the colored squares. I wasn't surprised by the largest stack.

On my desk was a multihued collection of worry, anxiety, and stress. These three words are a never-ending chorus of repetition from Christian women, no matter the setting.

Proverbs 3:5 says, "Trust in the Lord with all your heart..." *I know I'm supposed to trust God with all my heart, but it seems complicated at times. How can I trust Him when I'm stressed? How can I stop stressing so I can trust Him?* Do these questions belong to you?

Mom made my lunch on school days. At times, a

handwritten note would show up on the napkin. A scribbled affirmation or declaration of love. Once, I recall emptying the brown paper bag, the napkin fluttering away. A friend picked it up and began to read. *Ellen, Proverbs 3:5&6, Love, Dad*

Hey! How did he get to my lunch? Mortified, I thought, "Is he trying to further ruin my reputation?" You see, a boy had flirted with me, he was interested in me, and had recently called my house. And this boy was sitting at my lunch table. Yes, I had a reputation to protect. What if he called again and my dad answered his usual way? "Hello, Jesus loves you!" Stressed, I made it a top priority to beat my dad to the phone. Such embarrassment! The boy called that night and my dad beat me to the phone. Ugh! Stressed! Snotty, teenaged Ellen knew Proverbs 3:5, but wasn't willing to submit to its authority or author.

Why is this happening to me? Have you asked this before? Rebekah is a woman overcome by stress who understands trusting in the Lord. She bounced back and forth between wholly trusting God and having holes of anxiety attached to her heart.

One word sums up the struggle to completely trust God: control. We are captivated by control, dazzled with delight when we're in charge. We like control. The problem is, we're not good at it. We're inconsistent, unreliable, and untrustworthy.

One word offers the corrective: submit. Rebekah experienced peace when she submitted her life to God's will, God's way. *Why is this happening to me* was far from her thoughts.

Before we take a closer look at Rebekah's stressful situation, it's necessary to know the backstory. Abraham and Sarah raised Isaac. Sarah has died. Genesis 24:1 says, "Abraham is now old and well advanced in years." He was 100 when his son was born. To me, that's old. Isaac has become a man, and Abraham is *now old.* Can one be older than old?

It's time for Abraham to fulfill a responsibility - find a wife for Isaac. It's imperative the chief servant charged with this mission knows the expectations. Details are found in Genesis 24:1-4. She may not come from anywhere in Canaan where Abraham dwells. Yes, it's the promised land, but they haven't taken ownership. The people living in Canaan do not serve Abraham's God, so his son may not marry any of their girls. She must come from Abraham's hometown.

The chief servant has a question: "What if the woman is unwilling to come back with me? Shall I take Isaac there?" [Genesis 24:6-8] Questioning authority and asking authority a question are different. This submitting servant, desiring to fully submit to his master, asks a question which needs clarification.

Abraham was insistent. "Do not take my son back there...Jehovah, Elohiym, will send His angel before you." He trusts the Ruling, Existing One has gone before. What a beautiful display of submission. Abraham submits to God. An angel submits to God, going ahead of Abraham's servant and taking care of the details.

KEY POINT: TRUSTING GOD MEANS ENTRUSTING THE DETAILS TO HIM

This chief servant is used to being in charge. He's used to ordering order. To do his job well, he would need to be a detailed planner. A successful mission would require careful planning. Maintaining control, being in control, and being a controlled leader make him a successful servant. The time comes when the most careful planner must entrust the unknown and unforeseen details to God.

In Genesis 24:12 Abraham's servant teaches us how to entrust what we don't know and what we can't see to the Ruling, Existing One. He went as far as he could, obeying his master's directive, journeying to Abraham's hometown of Nahor, stopping at a well to water the camels. *Then he prayed.* Submitting requires praying. His attention is fully on God and His authority. Submitting to God doesn't come naturally, it takes intentionality.

When the servant submitted to God, eyes fixed and

focused on God's will, he could see God's way. It was evening, the time when women went to draw water, and this servant prays, "Give me success, show kindness." He entrusts the details to God. And then he actively participates in the plan. He doesn't take over; he willing inserts himself, submitting himself, entrusting himself to the plan an angel of the Lord previously set in motion.

As he's praying, a plan is formed. How sweet would it be for the very girl God chose for Isaac to come next to him, and when he asks for a drink responds with, "Drink this, and I'll water your camels, too." That's quite the plan. Remember, she must also be a relative of Abraham.

Genesis 24:15 begins, "Before he had finished praying..." I love when God surprises His followers. Like the thrill that comes when "Surprise!" is unleashed from those who kept mum regarding your birthday celebration.

Amen hadn't come, and the surprise was already approaching. He either prayed with his eyes open or God nudged them open. Continuing Genesis 24:15, "Rebekah came..."

Meet Rebekah, the grandniece of Abraham and Isaac's first cousin, once removed. Do not get stuck on the familial relationship. It's what they did, and it was acceptable to God's will being accomplished. If she agrees to give the servant a drink and offers his camels water, I'm high-fiving God all day long!

The servant makes haste, hurrying to meet her, and asks for a drink. Genesis 24:18-19 says, "Drink, my lord, I'll draw water for your camels, too." What?! Another surprise. Yay, God! Holy high fives happening here!

As a mom, I have a certain amount of control regarding my kids. The two youngest still need me controlling portions of their lives...the clothes they wear, the food they eat, the shows they watch, their bedtimes, the arrival times to practices and lessons, and the managing of their day-to-day activities. A great deal of their life is under my authority. And it's supposed to be.

Until they're older. The day will come when I'm no longer in control of their development, discipline, or decisions. Like my four older children, I will simply be their mother, no longer needing to mother them. Submitting to this order is necessary to maintaining a relationship with my adult children. I've had to have many conversations with myself reminding me to back off and be quiet.

In 2016, I was struggling as a mom to relinquish control. My kids weren't aware; it was an internal struggle. One day, I was praying for my kids and before I finished praying, before the amen was spoken, the Lord revealed six words, one for each of my kids. Six words beginning with 'C' were assigned to each of my children: clarity, choices, conviction, confidence, covenant, and contentment.

Contentment was assigned to Eric. He had begun a career in the corporate world putting his finance degree to work. He was also engaged to be married until his fiancée returned the ring and they parted ways. It's difficult to watch your kids hurt. It's imperative, though, that a mom of adult children be a sideline observer, no longer in the parenting game, but only the parent.

I did alright – until I inserted myself, uninvited, to the parenting game. Desiring only to offer words of comfort, they didn't land as I had planned. It was my eldest, Christine, who confronted me with words of wisdom I will never forget. "Momma, Eric has many friends, but he only has one mom – and he needs you to be his mom, not his friend."

It was necessary for me to heed Christine's advice; otherwise, my heart was susceptible to shame taking residence where the peace that passes all understanding desires to rest. Submitting the pieces I'd rather control allows the peace of Jesus to invade my hurting heart. When God revealed the word contentment, I had no idea how applicable it would be to Eric's life. It was not my responsibility to know, rather just trust.

KEY POINT: SUBMITTING TRUSTS GOD SEES WHAT YOU CANNOT

God went before this mom and saw what I couldn't see. Trusting Jesus for what we can't see protects us, sustains us, and prepares us as we submit to God's will, God's way. You may not see God's hand at work, but you can trust it's moving when you're submitted to Him.

Being on the sidelines allowed me a perspective I couldn't have if I was too emotionally close to Eric. A few months after the break-up, Eric called. We spoke often, but something was different as he said, "Momma, I'm not content." Remaining on the sidelines, I quietly cheered without Eric knowing. What kind of a mom cheers when her son admits he's not content?

The mom who's submitted to the Lord and praying contentment over her son. Immediately, awareness was a gift from the Holy Spirit. Discernment, through prayer, was like having a panoramic view of his current reality.

Genesis 24:21 reveals, "Without saying a word, the man watched..." If I was the servant, I would have begun putting everyone to task beginning with Rebekah, exclaiming, "Freeze!" and turning to one of my helpers demanding, "You, get the camels ready" and to another, "You, organize the entourage. We have places to go and people to meet!" This man silently watched as God's hand moved. A submitting servant waited for God's directive and listened for His voice. After all, God's in charge.

When the servant was finally compelled to inquire of her family and heard she was related to Abraham, he responded by worshiping Jehovah Elohiym. The Ruling, Existing One ordered this marvelous and surprising display.

KEY POINT: RECOGNIZING GOD'S WILL AT WORK COMPELS WORSHIP

Not only was she a relative of his master, but Rebekah said her family would provide rest and shelter for the servant, his crew, and their camels. Genesis 24:26 says, "Then the man bowed down and worshiped the Lord." A submitting servant recognizes and worships the One who ruled over the meeting before it happened and will provide as His will continues to unfold.

After disclosing the details and his intentions to Rebekah's family about why the servant was there, her father and brother responded. Genesis 24:51 records, "Here is Rebekah; take her and go, and let her become the wife of your master's son, **as the Lord directed**." [emphasis mine]

Defined, to submit means to yield, to give up to an authority; surrender; relinquish. Rebekah's family also submits. They aren't giving her up. Rather, they readily give her over to God's plan because they know He has directed this whole turn of events.

If you read all 67 verses of Genesis chapter 24, you won't find one distraction from God's will unfolding. Rebekah's mom doesn't assert her voice, declaring, "Over my dead body will you take my daughter so far away from our home." She did, however, ask for a little more time with her daughter. [see Genesis 24:55]

KEY POINT: GODLY PERSPECTIVE MUST KEEP YOUR ATTENTION

If Rebekah's mom asserts her motherly rights, she'll miss what's truly going on with her daughter. Her focus is incapable of seeing beyond the present, so she must trust God's perspective. Asserting her rights may halt, hinder, or hurt the will of God. A follower of Jesus follows. Period. A follower submits to God's will. Period. God has taken into consideration her feelings, He's fully aware of her mother-heart condition that thinks, "What's a few more days in the grand scheme of forever?" Spiritual perspective should have her attention. God has made His will for Rebekah abundantly clear. Hey, mom, submit to that.

Rebekah's family does something countercultural in response to the servant asking not to be delayed any longer. In Genesis 24:57 they allow her an opinion, "Let's call the girl and ask her about it." (I wonder if they thought she'd choose to stay home those extra ten days.)

Rebekah's response is further testimony of submission to Providence and His plan for her life. Genesis 24:58 records her response. *I will go.* That's different than *I will leave.* Going follows God and is focused on what lies ahead. Leaving is focused on what's left behind. This girl isn't leaving anyone or anything, she's following the Lord, and this perspective has her attention.

This is not a "Red Rover, Red Rover, send Rebekah on over" game. No one is forced to submit – submission is a choice. And God encourages it. More accurately, He demands it; therefore, it's a matter of obedience. James 4:7 exhorts, "Submit yourselves, then, to the Lord."

The word *then* has me backing up a few verses. In James 4:1-5 the pronoun *you* is penned sixteen times, suggesting a selfish perspective. For Rebekah, her primary concern is obediently following God by submitting to Him. No other person, including herself, should have precedence over Jehovah's will. Rebekah was all-in and three simple words support this.

I will go. What three words are needed for you to submit? I will stop? I will forgive? I will love? I will obey? I will submit? I will _____?

After Eric shared he was discontent and I silently cheered, like Abraham's servant, I didn't say a word. That doesn't mean I hung up on him and avoided any further conversation. Instead, I listened, told him I loved him, and prayed for and with him.

A few weeks passed. I accompanied my son on his visit to the seminary he would later attend. Who could have known discontentment was God going before Eric and calling him to a spiritual transformation, a different vocation, and a geographic change?

Eric was on the campus of Asbury Theological Seminary for only a couple days when across the way, he noticed a girl. Surprise! Unexpectedly, he was taken aback. Noticing a girl was not on Eric's agenda. Ok – noticing a cute girl is an ordinary part of a single guy's life. Eric was at seminary because, like Rebekah, when God called he responded with *I will go.*

A bigger plan was set in motion *before* Eric moved to Kentucky. Noticing this girl was a part of the yet-to-be revealed plan. Contentment filled Eric's heart when he submitted to God's call. Falling for a cute girl was an additional surprise from our good God.

Isaac and Rebekah meet face to face. Genesis 24:67 says, "She became his wife, and he loved her and was comforted by her." Though submission to His will supersedes human love, God certainly surprised this couple with their immediate connection and affection.

Eric and Rebecca – yes, how precious is that? - met face to face a couple of days after he noticed her. Rebecca has her own surprising story of how God called her to seminary. Similarly, education was her agenda – she wasn't expecting God to reveal a plan that included a man. Surprise! Ten months after meeting, Rebecca became Eric's wife. Isaac loved his Rebekah and Eric truly loves his Rebecca. And now there is contentment for my son, as he submits to a good God who has Eric's attention.

KEY POINT: SUBMITTING IS NOT VOID OF TROUBLE

We're halfway through this chapter, and shame hasn't been mentioned. When a follower is fully submitted, there is no space in the places of her heart for shame to attach. Jesus himself said, "In this world you will have trouble." [John 16:33] If I had to choose one thing I love and appreciate about God's Word, hands down it's His straightforward style.

"In this world, you will have trouble." That's straight talk - straight from God's heart to ours. All too often, followers of Jesus believe He's difficult to understand. We've been deceived to believe His word requires degrees, pedigrees, or referees. Untrue. Reading, knowing, living, understanding, loving, and following God's Word requires a willing, ready, open, and pliable heart. Not one word exists just for education, but every word is His revelation to you.

Jesus is in you. Trouble is in this world. He goes on to say, "...but take heart! I have overcome the world." Therefore, you can take courage, stand firm, and submit to the one who overcomes the world.

What happens when a submitted follower is overtaken by trouble? Not only is Rebekah an example of how to take heart and submit, she's also our illustration of being overtaken by trouble.

Rebekah and Isaac settle into life together. Genesis 25:21 reveals a husband who prayed for his wife. He prayed for 20 years regarding her barrenness. Through Sarai, we saw the disappointment, discouragement, and stress induced from this unmet expectation. Rebekah's story is no different.

Rebekah was an *I will go* woman. Her act of obedience did not remove future trouble from her life. As a woman with unmet expectations, she is in jeopardy of shame moving in. Stress stirs up shame.

Rebekah's declaration of submission should also be a testimony of how she'll react to future trouble. Proverbs 3:5-6 says, "Trust the Lord with all your heart...in all your ways acknowledge Him." All includes everything - any trouble, any disappointment, any crisis, any confusion, any discouragement, or any sadness. Any *thing* that attempts to interrupt our submission requires we trust the Lord with our whole heart. A follower of Jesus must acknowledge the Lord's presence through whatever trouble attempts to suspend her relationship of submission.

Trusting the Lord with your whole heart trusts Him when the holes are deep. Barrenness was a deep, stressful hole for Rebekah, so Isaac prayed on her behalf. Genesis 25:21 says God answered his prayer. Isaac knew the promises of God; Abraham made sure of it. Isaac was chosen to carry and pass on the covenant established with his father. Isaac trusted God and remembered His promise.

God answering Isaac's prayer is not Isaac getting what he wants - it's God providing what He promised. Rebekah is pregnant with twins. Pregnancy is stressful and instigates changes - physical changes, emotional changes, and appetite changes.

When a pregnant woman wants, needs, a chocolate shake from White Castle at 12:30 a.m., she expects a chocolate shake -

from White Castle. Burger King or McDonald's simply will not do.

So, when her husband returns from this midnight field trip, fulfilling his pregnant wife's must-have-or-someone-will-die expectation, and finds his beautiful bride sound asleep, after he drove the extra miles to the open White Castle, then you can be assured he woke her up – all 8-months-pregnant her – up! Imagine his shock (horror? disbelief?) when she took a few slurps from the straw, rolled over, and went back to sleep. Goodness, I tell this story as if I was the pregnant wife. (Kevin Harbin, I do love you for many things...that chocolate shake episode included.)

Shame knocked on Rebekah's heart's door as she uttered the question so many women ask when stress provokes anxiety: *why is this happening to me?* [see Genesis 25:22] It may appear she asks a good question. A submitting woman needs to be careful when asking why questions. Do you ask why because you don't get what you want? When life doesn't make sense, do you ask why? When life is hard or unfair, is why nearby?

Omitting the last two words in the question changes the intent. Asking "Why is this happening," keeps a follower's eyes firmly fixed on Jesus, whereas "Why is this happening *to me*," has her gaze on herself, with shame taking its spot in her heart.

Motive matters when questioning God. You can ask, but His answer could increase your stress level, raise anxiety, with shame putting down roots. There are times when the answer to your questions is wait. What an exasperating word. Wait – even its homophone is weight. Both are stress inducers.

God requires we wait, not to upset, provoke, or cause stress. His reasons vary, each circumstance different. But He also doesn't leave us wondering how to wait. One resource references 29 verses in the Bible with the word wait. Wait on the Lord. Wait continually. Wait patiently. Wait all day. Wait until the Lord comes. Wait eagerly. Wait expectantly. Psalm 27:14 says, "Wait for the Lord, be strong, take heart, and wait for the Lord."

Rebekah asks her question and then seeks the Lord. If

you're to wait for Him, you should first seek him. Genesis 25:22 says, "So she went to inquire of the Lord."

To inquire means to seek, to consult frequently. He answers Rebekah, but it's certainly not what this new mommy expected to hear. Look at Genesis 25:23. "Two nations are in your womb, and two peoples from within you will be separated; one people will be stronger than the other, and the older will serve the younger." She asked why, and God answered.

KEY POINT: DON'T BE SHOCKED, BE READY

When you're faced with trouble, are you shocked at the news or are you ready to do what's necessary? Shocked means you'll most likely freak out and be stuck. Ready means you're in action mode. Did God answer her *why* question only to shock her and watch her get stuck?

God wants Rebekah to be prepared for any future issues stemming from these facts. Who delivered this news to Rebekah? Who told her there are two nations in her womb? Who delivered the news she will deliver twin boys who will be at odds with one another throughout their life? The answer matters.

God, the Lord Jehovah, delivered the news. He allowed this barren momma to be pregnant with the battling boys He designed and created. Sometimes life is hard. Sometimes God's answer is not for what you hoped. Sometimes what we thought was difficult was only a stepping stone to a larger challenge. Shock and freaking out has us focused on the news, stuck and stammering, "why, Why, WHY?"

Being ready focuses you on the bearer of the news. Jehovah bore the news to Rebekah. Who is Jehovah? Answer this question. Jehovah is the Existing One. He exists for you, but how? Is He your provider, sustainer, rock, healer, refuge, joy, strength, fortress, redeemer?

In one of the churches my husband served as pastor, banners hung in the sanctuary bearing different names for God. Not an exhaustive list, each banner had Jehovah followed by a name bearing how He exists. Jehovah Jireh, God exists as provider. Jehovah Rapha, God exists as healer. Jehovah Shalom, God exists as peace. Jehovah Ra'ah, God exists as shepherd. Jehovah Shammah, God exists – He's present.

These banners spoke to me every time I entered that sanctuary, reminding me about certain aspects of God. Not only does He exist, He has all we need to face any trouble. Knowing and trusting who God says He is prepares you to be ready when rough and tough news is delivered.

The day came when God answered Rebekah's prayer – she's pregnant. He also answered her *why* question. However, the answer didn't meet her expectation. Now what? Did God make a mistake? No, He's incapable of error. The Existing One is Sovereign, having supreme rank and final say. God has a plan that includes and necessitates Rebekah submitting, being ready and prepared for what He's revealed. But Rebekah gets stuck.

Genesis 25:28 says, "Isaac loved Esau, but Rebekah loved Jacob." If you've never heard this story, this verse is a bullhorn broadcasting a heap of trouble. Listen up, Rebekah! You're in a place where shame will run rampant in your heart because you've reacted with shock instead of being prepared, ready to trust God – no matter what.

What occurs in Genesis 25:29-43; 27 & 28 is proof Rebekah was stuck from shock and not prepared. Take the time to read this story in full. Summarizing, God established a covenant relationship with Abraham to be carried through his bloodline and passed on until Jesus, the Christ, was born. This plan needed to begin somewhere with someone, and God chose Abraham. The nation of Israel, referred to as God's chosen people, is founded through this relationship. Because Isaac had twins, only one could continue what God started.

God chose Jacob. Why? Why did he choose the younger twin to be stronger, served by the older? Why? I'm a need-to-know kind of girl. But there are times when my need-to-know needs to be turned off. God chose Jacob. Period. He's God. He knows all; therefore, His plan must happen and will happen His way. Years later Jacob's name is changed to Israel. His grandma was told kings of peoples would come through her and she would be the mother of many nations.

God keeps His word. The most treasured King, Jesus, the King of kings, came from Jacob's bloodline. Now ask why God chose Jacob.

Rebekah made a poor choice when she chose to love one son over another. She made a mistake. Yes, she's human. Yes, she'll make mistakes. Yes, she'll make poor choices. Too many Christian women *help* other Christian women by defending their poor choices. Let's be clear and refrain from defending her – Rebekah sinned! And she'll have consequences because of it.

Love your Christian friends enough when they confess they sinned – leave it as a sin. Stop changing it to a mistake or poor choice. Confession prepares a follower to wholeheartedly follow Jesus. Rebekah loved Jacob and was more concerned with *helping* him get what he deserved than raising him to effectively carry covenant forward. And consequences resulted.

Jacob manipulates Esau to sell his birthright for a bowl of stew. God's will must be done God's way. Yes, Jacob is to have the birthright, but not through ungodly conduct. Rebekah overhears – ok, that's defending again – she eavesdrops on a conversation between dad and son. If she wanted to listen, she should have made herself known. Entering the room while clearing her throat would have sufficed.

A downward spiral has a beginning. A wrong direction begins with a step. Rebekah's spiral and misstep occurred years earlier. Standing at the door, eavesdropping, is a part of the spiral – not the beginning. Rebekah has opportunity to walk away. Choosing to stay separates her from her Lord.

KEY POINT: REFUSING TO YIELD, WIELDS YOUR WAY

Rebekah is no longer yielding to God. Her eyes are not fixed on her Lord because they're adhered to her selfish ambition and pursuit to get what she wants, what her son deserves. Chapter 27 outlines participation in deception devised from her wielding ways. To Jacob she says, "Listen carefully and do what I tell you." Rebekah neglects the opportunity to teach or remind her son what God told her before the boys were even born. She is so inwardly focused she incapable of guiding her son in the right direction.

Apparently, God wasn't working fast enough. Because He was too busy taking care of His other creations, she felt she needed to help Him out. She was deceived to believe she's not doing anything wrong devising, then wielding, her plans. Stress from not getting what she wants has her lending God a hand. God doesn't need you to help Him. You need to trust Him.

Rebekah had a pile of consequences from an avalanche of deception. Ultimately, things got so bad, her beloved son needed to leave and go far away from his brother who had murderous intentions. Wielding her ways culminated in shame residing in places of her heart that were once yielded and submitted to God. Rebekah trusted the Lord with all her heart until she was carried away by a question of why with stress influencing her to wield rather than yield.

KEY POINT: STANDING UNASHAMED STANDS FIRM IN YOUR FAITH

Rebekah wavered from God's ways when she wielded her ways. Submitting turned to living stressed. And it all began with the little questioning word *why*. A variety of things topple a woman from her firm foundation. Each of us is wired differently and what topples you may not budge me. What pushes me may not nudge you. Making the choice to stand firm on Jesus, submitting to Him, yielding to His ways is the only way each of us will stand firm.

I tend to stand firm when big trouble looms. For me, stress comes through the small trouble and shame threatening to take up residence in my heart. I negatively react to the smaller things and appropriately respond to the more significant issues. For example, as I've already shared, cancer and warts. Cancer was an overt and obvious issue to which I responded well. The ambiguity of warts had me discouraged, disappointed, and distracted – flawed reactions from a follower of Jesus.

Kevin was at the same seminary Eric now attends. We had four children under the age of five and this mommy needed a night out. Making sure Kevin and the kids were settled, I drove away in our minivan to meet my friend for dinner. We were praying this vehicle would last until Kevin graduated. I was ten miles from home when the minivan suddenly slowed and wouldn't accelerate about 25 mph.

The transmission was done. I drove the hilly backroads of Jessamine County, Kentucky and slowly returned home. "Well, Kevin, we have a praise-the-Lord-situation. We are now without a vehicle." I responded the same way I felt. Calm, cool, collected. We just lost our only form of transportation, and I was standing firm.

Compare that to the frantic, frenzied, furious woman who reacted weeks earlier to the windshield wiper flying off the same minivan during a storm. The thunder and lightning outside had nothing on the tempest inside. My children witnessed their mommy react with gale force emotion. *Why? Why now? Why me?*

I trust the Lord with a dropped transmission but stress when the windshield wiper dislodges - *why does that happen to me?* Move over yielding. Wielding has made room for shame, and it's knocking on the door of my heart. This time the door was wide open and shame walked right on in and took up residence due to my unacceptable reaction to a seemingly insignificant issue.

Some of you are thinking *gosh, Ellen, give yourself a break* or *everyone has a bad moment occasionally* or *you're only human* or *your reaction makes me feel better about mine.* Do not defend my outrageous temper-tantrum. Shame gets accommodated and tolerated when unacceptable reactions are disregarded. Satan takes opportunity to be forthcoming with our shortcomings, stealing joy, and determining identity.

As a follower of Jesus, choosing to stand firm in the faith submits to God's will and yields to His ways. Freed from the after-effects induced by stress is living as Jesus intends -

unashamed.

PONDER

deeply, carefully, and thoughtfully consider

1. Examine yourself carefully. How have you contributed to the stress in your life because you search for the answer to *why is this happening to me?*

2. Think deep and answer, what does it mean to submit?

PERSUADE
God's Word influences, encourages, and guides

1. Read Proverbs 3:5-6. What key words stand out, encouraging and guiding you away from anxiety and worry?

2. Rebekah waited 20 years before her prayer was answered. Submitting to God will require waiting. What guidance does God's Word have in regards to waiting? Psalm 27:14, Psalm 37:7, Hosea 12:6, Psalm 130:5, Micah 7:7, Lamentations 3:24-26.

PRACTICAL
applying Biblical Truth to present day

1. James 4:7 says, *submit yourselves, then, to God.* In Genesis 24:58, Rebekah's three words are, *I will go.* What is God asking of you? *I will* _____.

2. Read John 16:33. Two things vie for your attention: trouble and Jesus. Is your stress level associated with trouble? Describe how Jesus can have your full attention.

PERSONAL

inviting Jesus into your current reality

1. What's your motive when questioning God?

2. Trouble is a part of life. Stress does not need to be. What can you do to better prepare for potential trouble and avoid the shame of stress?

6

Rachel

my name is desperate and disappointed

One repeated thought making it into most of my speaking engagements will never grow old. It comes straight out of God's Word. Yet, it's one verse in the Bible that seems to be ignored. This one command, one mandate, one instruction, one life lesson, one area causes shame to be accommodated in many hearts. A lot of women – those who attend other churches, of course, are deceived to believe it must be tolerated.

As I mentioned in Chapter five, there is the stack of sticky notes gathered from the makeshift throne where ladies brought their giant issues to Jesus. Worry, stress, and anxiety were the top three. Worry and anxiety beat out parenting, marital, financial, career, and friendship issues.

Do you ignore the directive *do not be anxious*? If so, shame on you. Literally, shame moves into your heart when you ignore this mandate. Anxiety allows your heart to be Satan's playground, and he takes advantage.

I know God's Word says not to be anxious, but I can't help it. When Satan tramples, he confuses you with his deception. We've seen how he twists God's word. Did God really say *do not be anxious*?

Before you read on, answer this question. Did God really say *do not be anxious*? Perhaps what He said was *consider not being anxious*. Or, *it's ok to be anxious at certain times*. Maybe He said, *if you're a woman, then you can be anxious because you can't help it.*

Philippians 4:6 begins, "Do not be anxious..."

KEY POINT: THIS DIRECTIVE MUST BE TAUGHT UNTIL IT'S CAUGHT

In its original text, anxious means to not be troubled with cares. How in the world is a woman able to not be troubled with cares in this world? I'm so glad you asked.

But before I answer, I want to say I understand there are people who suffer from anxiety disorders. People I love are affected by this diagnosis. I am not negating or debating a doctor's diagnosis. I'm challenging followers of Jesus to take God at His Word. Whether you've been diagnosed or not, listen to the One who raised the dead to life and whose Son died to take away your shame...the shame from anxiety included.

Listen, and listen well. Because God has more to say on the topic. Continuing in Philippians 4:6 "Do not be anxious about anything..." Those last two words are crucial to the mandate. Is anything not included in anything?

In our home, we're not fans of the everything/anything things. You know – you've heard them – *he gets to do everything* or *I'm not allowed to do anything*. The everybody/nobody things aren't allowed either. *Everybody's doing it* or *nobody likes me*. Oh. My. Word. Somebody stop the insanity!

We think children are the only ones who have the everything/anything and everybody/nobody issues, but that is untrue! College-educated, capable, strong, feisty, bold, sweet, fun, caring women think, and sometimes speak, using similar clauses. The subject might change, but the theme remains. *Everything* causes anxiety. *Everybody* struggles with some form of anxiety.

Again, God is not difficult to understand. What in the directive, *do not be anxious about anything*, do you need defined or explained? When a passage is taught repeatedly, the struggle for it to get caught comes when we translate a mandate from God based on what we think, feel, or want. God's Word doesn't get reiterated by human emotion. His Word stands true on its own.

God understands humanity. He knows a woman's heart. He sees into all the hidden spaces and places where shame gets concealed. His mandate regarding anxiety protects your heart. Standing unashamed and firm in your faith requires living in a no-anxiety zone. Yes, when we all get to heaven what a day of rejoicing that will be – living in a no-anxiety zone awaits all followers of Jesus. But God's directives, commands, and instructions in the Bible are for today's living as well as tomorrow's promise.

Two measures that heighten anxiety are desperation and disappointment. Desperation is the state of being reckless from despair or hopelessness. Disappointment occurs when hopes are dashed. Hopelessness is common to both desperation and disappointment. Therefore, a loss of hope, a lack of hope, initiates anxiety and shame is introduced.

Rachel became desperate and disappointed. Unmet expectations, reckless decisions, and hopelessness turned to shame, determining her identity and stealing joy. Like most women, it took a long road for Rachel to get to a hopeless place. It's helpful to go to the beginning of her story and see the pieces that played a role in her shame.

KEY POINT: ALL SHAME HAS A STARTING POINT

Jacob. Remember him? The younger twin, beloved son of Rebekah, who needed to leave home because his brother wanted him dead. Jacob, chosen by God to be in a covenant relationship. Jacob, who was raised by God-fearing, God-serving, God-worshiping parents. Jacob, who wasn't raised in a perfect home. Who is? Deception and favoritism were two family strategies he learned from mom and dad.

Kevin and I are not perfect parents. We've made mistakes. We've sinned. How a follower of Jesus lands after a fall, is vital, especially in family dynamics. I've had to apologize and ask forgiveness of my children. I've had to admit to poor parenting strategies, failed attempts, grateful for re-dos a time or two, or 502.

We're also pretty sweet parents. Sweet, as in how a teenager says it, not flowery and candy-like. Some of our strategies are award-winning – that said with honesty, not pride. None are new to the world of parenting, I'm sure, but parenting six different personalities, temperaments, and dispositions require creativity on the parent's end.

Rachel's starting point involves Jacob.

When Jacob left, he fled to his mother's hometown, which happens to be the same place his grandfather left when God called Abraham into a covenant relationship that's always at the forefront of all events connected to Abraham and his descendants.

Though Jacob left his family, his father, Isaac, did tell him to go to his mother's hometown and find a wife among her relatives, specifically, his uncle's daughters. [Genesis 28:3-5] On his journey to his mother's hometown, God encountered Jacob in a dream. The message was clear – all people on earth will be blessed through you and your offspring – clear, yet overwhelming. Jacob needed to be reminded of the covenant which he had been called to participate in. God's voice went straight to Jacob's heart. He responded with a vow and sign of consecration. [Genesis 28:20-21]

Jacob arrived at Laban's home - his mother's brother, and was overjoyed to meet his extended family, especially Rachel, Laban's daughter, who was Jacob's second cousin once removed. (That's important information. Included in Isaac's blessing was Jacob marrying one of Laban's daughters.) Jacob works for no pay for Laban for a month. Laban then initiates a conversation regarding future wages.

Jacob negotiates a deal. Genesis 29:16-18 details the arrangement. Laban has two daughters, Leah and Rachel. This passage tells us a bit about each girl. Leah is older and, according to the writer of Genesis, has weak eyes. The King James Version of the Bible says, she's tender eyed – delicate, weak, timid – the meaning implies the same for her outward appearance.

Rachel is the younger sister, described as lovely in form and beautiful. Again, the King James Version reports she's beautiful and well favored. Rachel is gorgeous beyond words – inside and out.

Why does God do this? There we go, asking questions again that may be answered but are we prepared for it? Why does God create two completely opposite people and land them in the same family? One woman is gorgeous, and the other is not.

I remember a bumper sticker from years ago proclaiming, *God don't make no junk*. Grammatically botched, it tells truth. It's a crude way of making a point. All God's creations are good. He's incapable of making a disaster. It's not in His nature to make junk. As a good God, a creative God, all His designs are made from a good blueprint. Our human eyes see skewed. Human eyes notice weak, fair, lovely, beautiful.

The church in which I was raised in had a female pastor. She never married, and some said she was married to the church. Elsie was a great preacher, boldly proclaiming God's Word, preaching and teaching His truth. She was a powerhouse in the pulpit, pounding it harder than a muscled man. My dad and mom were saved under her preaching. If the writer of Genesis described Elsie, weak, frail, and homely could be words he used. Elsie's 4'9" frame made her appear weak, but her pulpit pounding showed otherwise. She didn't have a pretty face. It's true. Who cares? Elsie loved Jesus with her whole heart and that made her beautiful, gorgeous, in fact.

Jacob was in love with Rachel. Yes, she was beautiful, but she wasn't afraid of hard work, either. As a shepherdess, Rachel worked hard herding, caring for, and maintaining sheep. A job description might demand she be strong, determined, and hard-working, not afraid to get dirty, a regular ol' farmgirl. The arrangement was he would work for Laban for seven years in exchange for Rachel. Desire and love drove Jacob to make such an offer. He was a man intent on getting his girl. Shame had a starting point. Rachel would be disappointed in having to wait seven years. Yes, she had the man's love, but waiting seven years with him living so close would be disappointing.

Disappointment from dashed hopes can cause a girl anxiety. Determination to be patient would serve Rachel well.

For those who need the feel-good, sappy, romantic, chick-flick moment, you'll like Genesis 29:20, *So Jacob served seven years to get Rachel* (awww – but wait, it gets sappier)*but they seemed like only a few days to him because of his love for her.* I love a good romance, but this is a little much. Seven years is a long time.

When Kevin and I celebrated our seventh anniversary, we had four kids – 6, 5, 3, 1, and he was halfway through seminary. A lot can happen in seven years. In between Genesis 29:19 and 29:20 is a seven-year gap, with no recorded activity. We can assume Jacob worked and patiently waited for his opportunity to marry Rachel, his love.

In Genesis 29:21, Jacob expects Laban to keep his word, "...give me my wife. My time is completed, and I want to lie with her." Laban prepares a grand celebration and invites all the people from around to feast and enjoy the wedding reception. [Genesis 29:22]

KEY POINT: YOU REAP WHAT YOU SOW

As a follower of Jesus, are you aware this phrase is in the Bible? Paul wrote it in his letter to the church in Galatia. Galatians 6:7-8 says, "...do not be deceived, God cannot be mocked. A man reaps what he sows. The one who sows to please his sinful nature, from that nature will reap destruction..."

Years earlier, Jacob sowed deception toward his father. After he left his home, he had that dream where God confirmed His covenant with Jacob. Dealing with holes in your life is necessary for hearts to be made whole. Jacob has a hole. It needs confronting and filling.

Genesis 29:23 reports, "...when evening came, Laban gave his daughter Leah to Jacob, and he lay with her." Genesis 29:25 says, "... when morning came, there was Leah...Jacob says to Laban, why have you deceived me?" Oh, Jacob, a man reaps what he sows. God wasn't playing a sick joke on Jacob. God is confronting and filling a hole Jacob carried in his heart over seven years. God has plans for the one He is in covenant relationship with, and Jacob's sin of deception was in the way of him being used for God's purposes.

Leah's father deceived Jacob so she could be married. Laban's hometown custom said the older sister should be a wife before the younger sister. Besides, Jacob's love for Rachel was strong. Laban had no doubt Jacob still intended to take her as his wife. Jacob needed to finish Leah's bridal week, and then he could marry Rachel.

Shame has starting points. Rachel already waited through seven disappointing years. And now the man who has loved her equally as long has been given to her sister. Her hopes were dashed and her heart slashed through disappointment. Rachel has done nothing wrong. Why is she reaping disappointment, anxiety filling her heart, and shame beginning its descent?

KEY POINT: SIN BRINGS CONSEQUENCE

God is faithful, gracious, merciful, and His steadfast, never ceasing love will guard your heart when someone else's sin consequence affects your life. Rachel was experiencing this when Leah was given to Jacob. God's relationship with Jacob mattered. And Jacob's sin was a stumbling block to that relationship. Rachel was an innocent bystander, affected by the consequences. It was her safeguard to remember and trust what she knows about God before anxiety deceives her to believe a lie that potential shame must be tolerated.

Genesis 29:30 says Jacob loved Rachel more than Leah. This isn't an easy topic to write about or discuss. It's disgusting, really. Jacob's father did not model having more than one wife. Nowhere in Scripture will you find God condoning multiple wives. You'll find customs, expectations, and cultural standards supporting the practice. But man's custom, tradition, or culture does not mean it's God's intention or design. God will not bend His ways to societal conduct. He expects societies align their customs to His ways.

Jacob supports Laban's culture; therefore, consequence is a part of his future. Those in a covenant relationship with Holy God cannot exchange godly living and holiness for self-gratification and not expect correction, discipline, or consequence. Jacob has two wives and loves one more than the other.

Desperation is about to present and explode in Rachel. Anxiety will run rampant and shame will take up residence in her heart.

KEY POINT: AT TIMES, GOD DOES NOT IMMEDAITELY RESCUE YOU FROM DESPERATION AND BROKENNESS

Genesis 29:31 says, "When the Lord saw that Leah was not loved, he opened her womb, but Rachel was barren." Some may think since Leah has had to live in the shadow of her younger sister and was in a loveless marriage, God would give Leah children to somehow even the score. This kind of thinking is why we need God's truth as our guide. Before we start guessing what's going on, let's focus on the first phrase of this verse.

When the Lord saw that Leah... Before we read on, we must consider this beautiful reflection of Jehovah. The Existing One sees Leah. Jehovah sees all and knows all – He doesn't just have eyes on her situation. He has eyes on her heart, as well. As the lover of her soul, He inspects her heart. He isn't a cardiologist rescuing her from an attack. He observes, pays close attention, and carefully watches her heart's condition.

A few years ago, I got a phone call from my mom.

"What's up mom?"

"Oh, nothing, I think, well, maybe something. I feel weird. My chest feels heavy, like a lot of pressure is on it."

"Ok, let me talk to dad for a minute. Dad, you need to take mom to the ER. When you arrive, tell them it's her heart, and she'll get right in."

Later that night, it was confirmed she had a heart attack. The next day it was apparent she needed a quadruple bypass.

After her surgery, there was a team of medical personnel observing, paying close attention, and carefully watching the condition of her heart. They were charged with keeping her heart in rhythm, free from blockage, and effectively beating so her body could survive.

God's watchful care is over your soul, not the organ pumping blood. He desires to keep you in perfect rhythm, following His ways. He's aware of blockages that get in the way, and He's prepared to deal with them to save your life. God had His eye on Leah, and He knew the condition of her heart.

When the Lord saw that Leah was not loved, He opened her womb. What He did for Leah is not as important as Him noticing, carefully paying attention, and keeping a watchful eye on her. He didn't rescue Leah from her brokenness, He loved Leah in her desperation. His constant tender-loving care and consistent steadfast love holds her, keeps her, protects her through it all.

But Rachel was barren. Two broken-hearted, desperate sisters. Each has what the other wants. Rachel is troubled with cares. She cares for her husband, but shares him with his other wife, her sister. She desires to be pregnant, but she's barren while witnessing her sister give birth to four boys in a row. The Lord has His gaze on Rachel, too. He knows her heart; He sees her heart. He knows her desires; He sees her desperation.

But He's not ready to rescue her from her hurt. He desires for her to trust His presence as she hurts. Brokenness serves purpose. A follower of Jesus will be stuck when she views desperation as a blockage for God's redeeming work. Your desperate heart can take you straight to the everlasting arms of your Savior. As He hung on the cross, His arms were wide open welcoming all your brokenness and bearing your guilt and shame.

Shame no longer needs to be attached to you since it was nailed to the old rugged cross. Be desperate for His love and desperate for His forgiveness. He rescued you from the grip of sin. A broken, desperate heart my not be rescued right away. Trust Him. Only trust Him. A desperate heart does not need to associate with shame when you entrust your heart to Him and trust Him completely.

Details in the final section of Genesis chapter 29 inform us Leah has given birth to four boys. God opened her womb, and she's still dwelling in desperation. Desperate for her husband's love, she thinks now that she's bore him three sons, she'll have gained his love. The Lord sees her and He hasn't forgotten her. God is still at work in Leah's broken heart. He hasn't rescued her from her current reality but He's been present in it, a revelation Leah now recognizes. When her fourth son is born, she exclaims, "This time I will praise the Lord." The eyes of her heart were opened to the One who sees her.

Leah named this son Judah, another piece in God's redemptive plan. It's no coincidence Leah knew peace through the birth of this son. Our Savior, Jesus, the Prince of Peace is known as the Lion of Judah. A lion is fierce and powerful. Jesus fiercely loves you and is infinitely powerful.

KEY POINT: DESPERATION AND DISAPPOINTMENT: INTERNAL IGNITION, EXTERNAL EXPLOSION

Every time I read Genesis 30:1-8, I literally shake my head. I'm not shocked that God's people have such ridiculous behavior. I hurt that followers of Jesus feel the need to resort to such ridiculous behavior. This kind of stuff is smut novel worthy. Adding detail and dialogue, it would potentially be an R rated movie. But this is God's Word. This story is not included for us to dwell on the dirt. God's people majorly mess up, and we have lessons to learn from their mistakes.

Leah and Rachel each had a maidservant accompany them into their marriages. Zilpah was assigned to Leah and Bilhah to Rachel. Handmaids helped with household responsibilities and attended their designated mistress. Miss Maytag and Miss KitchenAid are our current handmaids.

Rachel was internally ignited each time her sister had another baby. Matched together, the dynamite duo of disappointment and desperation were combustible. Inflamed,

Rachel was bound to explode.

Genesis 30 begins, "When Rachel saw she wasn't bearing Jacob any children, she became jealous of her sister." Notice what has Rachel's attention. Whatever has your attention has you. If our attention is on what we don't have, disappointment reigns, anxiety heightens, and shame settles. Rachel's emotions are ruled by disappointment. Enter jealousy. Disappointment awakens resentment.

Continuing in Genesis chapter 30, "...she says to Jacob, 'Give me children, or I'll die!" Resentment fans the flame, casting blame. Now it's Jacob's fault she is barren. Rachel is blinded by flames incited from her selfish attitude. Is it wrong for Rachel to grieve? No. Is it wrong for her to hurt? No. Is it wrong for her to be disappointed? No. Grieving, hurting, disappointment are not sins. However, allowing them to burn inside her heart birthed desperation.

Desperate, Rachel explodes. Now disappointment and desperation are in charge, a dreadful duo. Rachel hands over her handmaid, Bilhah, to Jacob. The perhaps-I-can-plan of Sarai is attempted. Custom and culture said building a family this way was acceptable, God did not.

Jacob marries Bilhah. She conceives and gives birth to two boys for Rachel to name and raise. After the second boy is born, Rachel's jealousy incited a conflict between sisters, a duel. Rachel prevailed and overcame the struggle – so she said.

Leah would not concede. She stopped having children, so she arranged for Jacob to marry Zilpah, and she bore him two sons. This is not a battle between sisters. Shame has these sisters engaged in a struggle with disappointment and desperation.

Rachel's identity is determined by what she doesn't have and can't accomplish. She has not overcome. She has not prevailed. She has been ruled by these two destructive emotional reactions. Shame internally exploded, causing her to behave in ways she never imagined.

KEY POINT: A SURRENDERED HEART LIVES UNASHAMED

Rachel's rage simmered. Years passed and Jacob was the father of ten boys. Leah had six sons, Bilhah and Zilpah each had two. Genesis 30:22 says, "Then God remembered Rachel; He listened to her and opened her womb." God is not late. God didn't forget Rachel. Notice the three action words: remembered, listened, opened.

God remembered her - He thought of her. El-ohiym had Rachel on His mind. The Ruling One is now in charge of Rachel. She gave up. She relinquished control. Disappointment and desperation no longer determine her identity.

God listened to her – God hearkened to her. El-ohiym turned His ear to her. Rachel pleaded to The Ruling One and He was pleased. Rachel didn't tell God what to do, she shared her heart with the One who ruled it.

God opened her womb – the Ruling One allowed her to conceive. Rachel is no longer disappointed in what she couldn't have or accomplish. She surrendered desperation over to the One who rules her heart. What was once empty is now filled.

In Genesis 30:23 Rachel responds to God's incredible, amazing, beautiful grace exclaiming, "God has taken away my disgrace." What Rachel surrendered, God graciously took away. Disgrace is reproach, scorn – a condition of shame.

Did you catch that? Excuse me a minute, I need to jump up and down, exclaiming hallelujah! He took her shame. He took yours to His cross. Be desperate for Jesus and crave a compelling desire for His love, His grace - His will, His way. Surrendering your emptiness, unmet expectations, and disappointments to Jesus allows you to live unashamed.

PONDER
deeply, carefully, and thoughtfully consider

1. Thoughtfully, carefully, and honestly consider how you feel about Philippians 4:6. *Do not be anxious.* Do you pay attention to it? Do you avoid it? Is it attainable? How is it possible?

2. Has desperation and disappointment affected your walk with Jesus? Describe.

PERSUADE

God's Word influences, encourages, and guides

1. Read Philippians 4:6-7. Panic or peace? Chaos or calm? Anxiety or assurance? How does this passage influence your perspective?

2. Genesis 29 describes how disappointment and desperation were a part of Rachel and Leah's life. What encouragement do you find within this account?

3. Genesis 29:35 records Leah praising the Lord. What changed? What happened?

PRACTICAL
applying Biblical Truth to present day

1. 1Peter 5:7 should encourage anyone desperate and disappointed. [a] According to this verse, you have a responsibility, what is it? [b] How can Philippians 4:6 and 1Peter 5:7 get applied to shame residing in your heart?

2. Genesis 29:31 says, "When the Lord saw that Leah…" God has eyes for Leah AND her situation. Describe a time when you knew God saw you amid a desperate and disappointed circumstance.

PERSONAL

inviting Jesus into your current reality

1. Genesis 30:1-24 describes the external explosion caused by internal desperation. Verse 22 is a megaphone announcing God's grace showing up in the midst of Rachel's explosive disappointment.
   [a] What are you currently disappointed about?
   [b] What three things did God do for Rachel in 30:22?
   [c] Can He do the same for you?

2. Genesis 30:23 records God taking Rachel's shame. What needs to be surrendered in your life to live unashamed as Jesus intends?

7

Dinah

my name is mistreated

Secrets, we all have them – and we've been deceived to believe they should stay hidden. Secret drawers. Secret compartments. Secret hideaways. Secret confessions. Secret deodorant. Even Victoria has a secret, though not much is concealed.

Before I was married, I was involved in youth ministry. Teen girls had secrets. Some were willing to share. A girl began with, "I have a secret I want to share with you. Promise you won't tell anyone?" My ready response was, "I want to listen, but I can't make that promise. Will you trust me to carefully and properly handle your secret?" I was baffled that most chose not to divulge the secret. Apparently, they just wanted to reveal it, not deal with it.

Managing secrets well matters. Either you control them or they control you. Mistreatment is similar. Does a mistreatment from your past still manage you? I've been mistreated – most instances I've handled well. Some took time but were resolved and are no longer in control. Others, I didn't manage well and they took over, leaving shame in their wake.

Being mistreated by a friend is a deep wound, an experience I know firsthand. Mistreatment from church people – been there, done that, too. Violated? Yes. Abused? Yes. Nobody volunteers to be mistreated, violated, or abused. But chances are, most people have experienced one, if not all three.

Mistreatment can be subjective – what I classify as abusive, another may disagree. That's ok. Let's not allow that to get in the way of the message. I'm not a licensed counselor; therefore, I have no authority to diagnose or professionally counsel on the topic of abuse. The goal of this chapter is to teach how being mistreated causes shame. Yet, a follower of Jesus can live unashamed, no longer deceived to believe it must be tolerated. I desire to be sensitive regarding the topic of abuse. For anyone who's been abused, you're on a journey of healing. If you'd like guidance to help you manage the journey from a trusted source, someone who's lived it personally, my friend, Mary, writes and speaks on the topic. She's overcome much from her sexual abuse and is passionate for you to be redeemed and whole. You can find her at marydemuth.com.

Shame from any violation profoundly affects a follower of Jesus, burrowing into places of your heart. The Light of the World is waiting to reveal those spaces so you can live unashamed.

Too many Christian women keep secret shame a secret – even from themselves. Oh, they remember the act, but they'd rather keep the unsettling aftermath concealed. This, my friends, is why secret shame gets accommodated and tolerated, determining your identity and stealing your joy.

KEY POINT: JESUS KNOWS YOUR SECRETS

Nothing is hidden from the Lord. Jeremiah 23:24 records God asking, "Can anyone hide in the secret places so I cannot see him?" Yes, you can certainly keep your secrets hidden, but never from God. Psalm 44:21 concludes, "He knows the secrets of the heart." Because your hidden secrets are known by Jesus, He can be trusted with them as well. He knows the pain and heartache inflicted on you - Jesus knows. The inappropriate touch, Jesus saw. The verbal attacks, every hurled word, Jesus heard. The slap, the punch, Jesus felt the pain. The abandonment and neglect, Jesus was present.

Allowing shame to fester keeps you stuck on your faith journey. Mistreatment of any kind must be dealt with or it will surely mess with you.

God's Word is useful. 2Timothy 3:16-17 says, "All Scripture is God-breathed and is useful for teaching, rebuking, correcting, and training in righteousness, so that the man of God man be thoroughly equipped for every good work." A good work awaits you. Revealing the shame keeping you from faithfully following Jesus is part of equipping you for good work. Revealing shame is good work. Every word in the Bible is useful. Every story, profitable.

And that includes Dinah. Her story will teach us. It might correct and restore. It could improve character. Some will be rebuked, reproved – convicted. Dinah's story can also train us in righteousness – if we lay our hearts and minds open to the good work required to live unashamed.

Dinah is a sister and a daughter. Her parents are Jacob and Leah. Dinah has ten older brothers. I wonder how they felt when their baby sister was born. Was an immediate, protective nature embedded in them?

A few years ago, Sukanya received a gift that still adorns space on a wall in her bedroom. She unwrapped the piece of art on Christmas morning. The tag on the gift said *To: Sukanya, Love: your older brothers - Andrew, Eric, Troy, and Jaylen.* Though we have a picture to remember the moment, I can still recall it as if it were yesterday.

Sukanya is kneeling on the floor in her pink, polka-dotted pajamas. She's holding the present in her hands, her head is slightly tilted, and a sweet smile is on her face. It appears she thinks she's the only one in the picture. However, standing behind her are three adult brothers and one brother, a year older than she, all with serious looks on their faces. Their arms are crossed in front of them, legs slightly parted, standing their ground, ready for battle. *Note to all boys: I was born a princess and I expect to be treated like one* is the message she holds. Her brothers have taken their stand - mess with my sister, and you'll deal with me.

Jacob, his four wives and all their children have left Laban's home and are now living just outside the city of Shechem in Canaan. Some events in Jacob's life are necessary to mention because they connect to Dinah's story. Just before Jacob left Laban, God told him to go back to his home where his father and brother lived. If you recall, Esau wanted Jacob dead.

Wanting to obey God, Jacob carefully planned and prepared himself, his family, his servants, and flocks for the reunion.

One night, prior to the meeting, Jacob was alone and God met him there. A wrestling match occurred between Jacob and an angel of the Lord. This necessary struggle proved to Jacob God is in charge. If Jacob follows God's will, God's way, God will protect, provide, and guide Jacob's life. God gave Jacob a new name, Israel, reminding him to whom he belongs, who initiated covenant, and who intends to keep His word that nations, peoples, and kings would come through Jacob.

The reunion with Esau goes better than Jacob expected. As they part ways, Jacob tells his brother he needs to move slowly to protect the flocks and not push them too hard.

And that's when Jacob bought a plot of land from the sons of Hamor, the father of Shechem, and set up camp in view of the city the prince is named for, Shechem. God told Jacob to go back to his father's home. Why purchase a plot of land if you're not staying? Surely Jacob could have negotiated a lease or rental option.

Jacob settles at Shechem and builds an altar. This may seem righteous. However, Jacob can build 100 altars - since God didn't lead him there, he'll struggle to meet God there. God told Jacob to be elsewhere, yet Jacob lingers where God didn't lead.

KEY POINT: LINGERING WHERE GOD HASN'T LED INITIATES TROUBLE

Many in the Bible found this point to be true. King David remained at the palace at the time when kings and their men go off to war. He thought he was avoiding a skirmish, but the ensuing battle in David's life from his sin with Bathsheba was the result of his lingering.

We saw what happened when Abram and Sarai lingered in a place God had not led them. A heap of trouble surrounded them and many in Egypt, because of their disobedient trek.

Genesis 34:1 says, "Now Dinah went out to visit the women of the land." That's a problem - right there in the first verse of Dinah's story. Why is Jacob's daughter hanging out with the women of Shechem? Commentators believe Dinah is between 13-16 years old. Have you noticed or experienced teenaged girls? They don't always think things through. They're still maturing and need guidance on making wise decisions. Impulsivity and desires can block wisdom.

Dinah didn't go to the edge of town and observe; she wasn't content to glance from afar. Her desire was to look, see, and inspect the women of Shechem with an up close and personal inspection. Either she's visited before or she isn't shy. Her desire is to be included and involved with the other girls in Canaan. What will it hurt if she associates with the girls of Shechem? It makes perfect sense that her parents would have established boundaries for their young daughter. Though it's not recorded, it's possible she disobeyed her parents' rules about where she was allowed to be.

Sometimes, a girl just wants to have a little fun. What's wrong with that? According to the National Institute on Drug Abuse, 23% of those who try heroin will become addicted. What's wrong with a little heroin? In December 2016 a wildfire in Tennessee killed 14 people. Hundreds lost houses and more than 2400 structures were damaged or destroyed. All because two juveniles played with matches. What's wrong with a couple of kids playing with a little fire?

Those may seem exaggerated comparisons, but they make the point. Like the kids in Tennessee, Dinah was where she shouldn't have been. Even David's sin with Bathsheba resulted in the foolish and senseless death of others. Serious disease was inflicted on many Egyptians when Abram and Sarai went where God hadn't led. And Dinah is about to experience a horrific violence because her dad lingered, and she wasn't content to watch from a distance. She desired to linger where she wasn't allowed.

Genesis 34:2 reports, "when Shechem saw Dinah, he took her and violated her."

I can't read this without weeping. Dinah wanted to visit the girls of Shechem and while she's watching them, he's got his eye on her. Hers was an innocent desire; his look, possessive. As a mom of a young daughter, if I notice a boy looking at her like Shechem looked at Dinah, we'll be having a conversation.

The New International Version records, 1) Shechem saw, 2) he took her, 3) and violated her. The King James Version records, 1) he saw her, 2) he took her, 3) and lay with her, 4) and defiled her. A progression of horror led to Dinah being violated and mistreated. Concealed shame then took its hiding place.

Shechem saw Dinah. What's wrong with noticing a cute girl? Nothing. What's wrong with staring at a cute girl? Intention changes and alters behavior. Sports shows are viewed in our house often, especially when the older boys are home. From the time our sons were young, we taught them it was their responsibility to turn their head or close their eyes when inappropriately dressed women appear on the screen.

Swimsuit models and Victoria, with her unconcealed secrets, invade my home all too often. Innocently watching a game or TV program they appear, up close and personal in my living room, inviting male eyes to notice, even stare. How long is an average commercial spot? Most are 30 seconds – that's too long for a look. That constitutes a stare. A great deal of planning and decision-making can occur in that small space of time.

Shechem decided to make a plan and set it in motion when he saw Dinah. He took her. The word *took* has many meanings. He fetched her, seized her, snatched her, or carried her off. What he saw he wanted, and he would stop at nothing to get it. Why is Shechem hanging out where the ladies were anyway? Why Dinah? He's the prince of the land. He could have any girl he desired. And maybe he has. We don't know.

Shechem's plan continued. He lay with her and defiled her, he had sex with her and violated her. Disgusting. Horrific. Appalling. My stomach knots. Even as I type these words, I find I'm stopping and clinching my hands, making fists. Varying emotions bounce around in my head and my heart. Anger, sadness, frustration, grief, rage. Compassion causes me sympathy for Dinah. Some reading this can empathize by placing themselves in her predicament because they've experienced similar mistreatment.

Genesis 34:3 says, "His heart was drawn to her, he loved the girl, and spoke tenderly to her." Dinah has been mistreated, taken advantage of, violated. Shechem's assault on Dinah involved control, manipulation, and erratic behavior. He turned on the charm, talked sweet to her and declared his love for her. Defile is not love. Abuse is not love. Violation is not love. Mistreatment is not love.

Genesis 34:34 chronicles Shechem demanding, *get me this girl as my wife!* proving this prince is a piece of work. Apparently, he's allowed to snap his finger, boastfully demand anything from his daddy, the ruler of the land, and it will happen. *Get me* is the same as *he took her* – in other words, seize her, snatch her – whatever it takes, get this girl as my wife!

Genesis 34:5 says, "When Jacob heard Dinah was defiled, his sons were in the field with his livestock; so he kept quiet about it until they came home." Jacob is quiet, his emotions unmentioned. The brothers, however, were *filled with grief and fury.* [Genesis 34:7]

Shechem's father is manipulated by his son and carries out his demand. The ruler in the land has a manipulator for a son. Who's in control here? Obviously, the son, the manipulator. Both fathers, Hamor and Jacob, appear weaker than their sons.

Jacob's daughter has been violated, defiled, mistreated and he has a meeting with her abuser's father negotiating a marriage deal. Would someone please go and see to Dinah's well-being? She's a teen girl who's been assaulted and atrociously mistreated. She needs attention, compassion, and validation.

KEY POINT: ANYONE MISTREATED NEEDS VALIDATING AND DEFENDING

It's soothing to hear someone say, "I understand" or "I know what you're going through" or "Keep talking, I'll just listen" or "I am so sorry this happened to you." There are any number of sentiments or statements that can be spoken as a means of validating an incident that occurred and confirming the pain is real.

When someone has been violated, having a trusted source confront the attacker, the abuser, is vital toward them feeling safe and secure.

I was 12. My mom and I were in our yellow, wood paneled station wagon, her driving while I sat unusually quiet opposite her. My mom is naturally a sweet lady, but it was turned up a few notches as she spoke. "Ellen, I need to ask you a question, and I need you to be honest with me, honey" A wise mom has difficult conversations while in a moving vehicle.

"Ok," I sheepishly responded, face downcast, tears accumulating.

"It has come to my attention that grandpa touched you inappropriately. Is this true?"

How did she know? I hadn't told anyone what happened. Spending time at my dad's parents' house was something we often did. On a recent visit, I was in the basement playing at the pool table. Again, a common occurrence. Only something very uncommon occurred.

I was just about to go upstairs and my grandpa stepped in front of me and touched my chest. I was horrified. I remember frantically trying to back up so I could step around the old man and fly up the stairs. A distant commotion caused him to halt, and I bolted. Seconds later, I was in the safety of the kitchen near grandma.

A couple of days later, the confrontation in the station wagon occurred. Mom already knew the answer, but her gentle, yet firm, approach caused me to respond. Crying, I told her it was true.

I don't recall our destination as I'm sure there wasn't one. A conversation of validation was the objective. Mom reached her hand for mine and told me how sorry she was. She said she believed me, and she would be talking to my dad about the incident. She also said I was free to come to her anytime I wanted to discuss it further, if necessary. When we returned home, my parents went to their bedroom to talk. Moments later dad emerged with a look I've not seen in his eyes before. It was an intersecting of compassion and anger – and I had no doubt what part was for me.

Dad held me and told me he loved me and was sorry. He said he was proud of my honesty, and then he was gone. Mom said he was going to grandpa's. At 12, that was all I needed to know. Years later dad shared with me about that night he confronted his father.

My father is a gentle man. I have never heard him raise his voice at my mom. I've never heard a cuss word escape his lips. Passion is in my dad. He reserves it for certain things, like worshiping Jesus and Detroit Tiger baseball games, mostly. Dad can get demonstrative over both, especially in a worship gathering. Now in his 80's, it's not as overt as it was, but what a joy it is to watch my dad praise Jesus as he sings louder and more distinctly than most demonstrating an outpouring of his love for his Savior.

Dad shared with me he had a passionate talk, fueled by anger, with his father. I felt defended, safe, and secure with my dad about the episode that forever changed my relationship with grandpa. To the day he died, I was never around him unless someone else was present. My dad told me I could call the shots regarding grandpa. If I didn't want to hug, touch, or be near him, I didn't have to be. I chose to keep a physical distance. Grandpa broke trust, and I implemented boundaries because my parents validated and defended the despicable act.

The negotiation regarding Dinah began: *my son has his heart set on your daughter. Please give her to him as his wife.* You've got to be kidding me! It continues, *intermarry with us; give us your daughters and take our daughters for yourselves. You can settle among us; the land is open to you. Live in it, trade in it, acquire property in it.* [Genesis 34:9-10] Absolutely ridiculous! Allowing this negotiation to become reality would create opportunity for continued violations. Dinah's situation alone is enough reason for the Jacob family to bid farewell to the Hamor family and start packing the camels, gather the herds, and hightail it to where they were supposed to be. Family secrets are common. Regrettably, they exist. And they're powerful enough to damage a family. Yet, left unspoken, shame will control the abused, while the abuser pretends nothing happened and sadly continues to perpetrate despicable acts. Those mistreated need secrets exposed.

Leaving secrets in the dark is another playground offering opportunity for Satan to trample on shame-filled, fragile hearts. Shine the Light of the World on the shame, and Satan will scurry away.

Women who have been mistreated share a shame difficult to confront. They did nothing wrong, but shame festers anyway. Some abusers are dead, some are unknown, some can't be found. How can a mistreated woman deal with shame when she can't confront the one to blame?

Mistreated women struggle with the desire to get even. After all, abusers should pay for what they've done. Oh, dear friend, don't allow this to consume you. Longing for retaliation, vengeance, and revenge adds shame. It, too, badgers and make things worse.

KEY POINT: SHAME INHABITS YOUR HEART THROUGH RETALIATION, VENGEANCE, AND REVENGE

Complete the phrase: two _____ don't make a _____. If you inserted wrongs and right, you're correct. This is an old proverb dating back to the 1700's. Someone who has done something unjust or dishonest has no justification for acting in a similar way. Dinah's brothers need to know this.

Genesis 34:7 conveys her brothers are filled with grief and fury. Literally, they're hot! They saw her violation for what it was - a senseless, immoral, profane disgrace done to their sister. And they're livid, enraged. The brothers listen to Hamor and Shechem's negotiation, but they aren't buying any of their manipulative jabber.

In Genesis 34:11-17 the brothers spoke their deceptive plan: *become circumcised and they'll agree to join bloodlines with you*. God's ways must be followed His way. Circumcision was not theirs to finagle. Yes, they're filled with fury, and they should be, but when God's people want retribution, they'll continue to suffer with shame.

The Canaanites become circumcised, using a sacred ceremony for sinful purposes. Circumcision was a sign of covenant relationship marking men as set apart for God. A sign they're ready to be used by God. Jacob's sons did not have the right to use circumcision as means for retaliation.

Filled with grief and fury reacts and doesn't consider the consequences. These brothers got their revenge. Righteous anger, right? Wrong. Throughout this whole account, God is not mentioned. Dinah has been mistreated, abused, and the men in relationship with God are absent from the altar. Neglecting God causes out of control fury and what appears to be a victory born from extreme vengeance.

Shechem was wrong. Simeon and Levi, Dinah's brothers were, too. Two wrongs, not one right. If Dinah were to speak to her situation today, what would she say to those who have been abused or mistreated? Would she testify to God's unfailing love? Would she say though she didn't choose the horrific act done to her, she certainly had a choice how she reacted to it?

A mother faces the man who kidnapped, abused, and murdered her daughter. She looks him straight in the eye and forgives him. How? She acknowledged God and refused to allow revenge to rule her heart.

A man is wrongfully convicted of first degree murder. While in prison he comes into a personal relationship with Jesus. Years later his conviction is overturned. The reporter telling his story asks how he could forgive the ones who wronged him, mistreated him. He says Jesus is the only one who can bring any sense or peace to such a circumstance.

A young lady stands on a stage telling how she is the result of her mother being gang raped. Her mother never saw abortion as an option. Instead, she prayed her child, though conceived through an evil act, would one day be used by God in mighty ways to help draw others to Jesus.

At sixteen, a Christian young lady gave in to pressure and had sex with her boyfriend. She knew it wasn't right; she should wait for marriage. The relationship didn't last. Years later she marries another man but continues to be badgered with the shame of her premarital choices. She was deceived to believe it must be accommodated and tolerated in her heart.

But the Lover of her Soul loved her completely. He gently exposed her responsibility in the mistreatment and the shame left behind. Jesus revealed she must repent and claim the promises of His Truth every day for shame to no longer badger her heart.

Though the stories of mistreatment change, how a follower of Jesus deals with the hidden shame does not. Jesus is the only true source of healing and wholeness. His light goes directly to shame burrowing in your heart, His redeeming work begins.

PONDER
deeply, carefully, and thoughtfully consider

1. Go to the deep places of your heart and consider what secret remains concealed. Are you tired of it dealing with you? Are you ready for it to be revealed?

2. If you've suffered any mistreatment, carefully consider how the shame from it affects your relationship with Jesus. Describe.

PERSUADE
God's Word influences, encourages, and guides

1. Read Jeremiah 23:24 and Psalm 44:21. How are you encouraged by these verses? Is there an area of your life that needs to be influenced by these verses?

2. In Genesis 32:9, as Jacob prays he acknowledged that God had told him to go back to his hometown. In Genesis 33:18 he purchases a plot of land nowhere near his hometown. In Genesis 33:20 Jacob set up an altar on the plot of land. Based on this progression, discuss the difference between doing God's will your way and doing His will, His way.

PRACTICAL
applying Biblical Truth to present day

1. According to Genesis 34:7 and 34:25-29, Dinah's brothers acted in retribution. Look up Deuteronomy 32:35 and Romans 12:17-19. How can you apply these passages to your life if you've been mistreated?

2. Jacob lingered in a land where God hadn't led and it initiated trouble for his family. Are you lingering in a place where God would never lead? [i.e. unforgiveness, bitterness, resentment, jealousy, pride, laziness, etc.] What lesson can you apply to where you may be lingering?

3. 2Timothy 3:16-17 says *all Scripture is useful*. How is Dinah's story useful to you?

PERSONAL
inviting Jesus into your current reality

1. Read 1Corinthians 1:3-4.
    [a] How is God described?
    [b] How often are you comforted by God?
    [c] In vs. 4, two words denote purpose - *so that*.
       What's the purpose?
    [d] Can you trust your secrets and/or mistreatment
       to the Father of compassion and God of all
       comfort?

2. Who is a trustworthy source where you share your
    deepest hurts? What needs to be revealed so the
    shame left by the hurt no longer has access to your
    heart?

8
Potiphar's Wife
my name is manipulator

When my daughter, Sukanya, was six, she would often declare, "Mommy, ladies shouldn't 'nipulate, cuz 'nipulation is wrong." My older daughter, Christine, and I drilled this fact, this life lesson, into that sweet six-year-old. Today, at 12, if you were to ask Sukanya, "what two things are unacceptable for Harbin ladies" she'd respond, "negotiation and manipulation." You might think she answered a tad snotty. But it's her current middle-school-girl doing the eye-roll, head bent, hand on hip - her demeanor hinting you asked a question to which you already knew the answer.

Oh, my daughter knows the answer, but this middle-schooler is still in training to be a non-negotiating, non-manipulating lady. I give her breaks – not excuses – cutting her some slack as she prepares and I guide her to be a lady who stands unashamed, freed from the shame manipulation lands in a woman's heart.

Though I will continue to train, teach, and guide my daughter to become a woman who doesn't manipulate, ultimately, it's her choice. I pray she chooses right and well.

Defined, manipulation means to manage or influence skillfully; to adapt or change to suit one's purpose or advantage. (dictionary.com) Every time a teacher needs to gain control of her classroom, she causes the students to adapt to her standards. That's manipulation. Is it wrong?

A mother and father go to a congressional hearing to testify how their child was killed by a drunk driver. Their desire is to skillfully influence politicians to consider changing or amending laws holding the drunk driver accountable for his actions. That's manipulation. Is it wrong?

A pregnant woman has a breech baby in her womb. The doctor twists, turns, and attempts to change the position of the unborn baby. That, too, is manipulation. Is it wrong?

No. But there's one word imbedded in the definition that needs a spotlight. *One*. To change or adjust to suit *one's* purpose. This implies motive. Within these examples the teacher, grieving parents, and the doctor have appropriate motive.

KEY POINT: MOTIVE MATTERS

Manipulation is a sure way to attain the goal of getting what you want, suiting your own purpose, expecting others to adapt or change to you. When our focus is on me, myself, and I, it's imperative one purpose gets suited. But which one? Me, myself, or I? Manipulation takes a lady on roads she never imagined traveling. Rough terrain, massive roadblocks, deep potholes on life's journey can contribute to shame; therefore, motive matters.

Scores of Christian women would deny being manipulators. But let's not look at scores of other women; instead, look in the mirror. Go ahead, find a mirror, look closely at the one looking back at you. Do you see one who manipulates, or do you see a manipulator? Knowing which describes you best, the noun or the verb, matters to motive. Do you manipulate, or are you a manipulator?

There is a difference. A manipulator manipulates as a lifestyle. Infrequent manipulating occurs when frustrated women choose it as their default method. However, when tolerated, both determine identity and steal joy. Neither allows you to stand unashamed. Both hinder relationships with others and keep you stuck on your walk with Jesus.

Somewhere in a manipulator's past, manipulating worked. And when practiced often, the expectation others would adapt and change to suit her desired outcome was successful. It takes repetition to become a master manipulator – manipulation rehearsed to perfection. If awards were presented, Potiphar's wife would be decorated for her many performances.

Genesis 39:7 says, "After a while, his master's wife took notice of Joseph..."

his = Joseph
master = Potiphar
wife = Potiphar's wife
Joseph = Jacob's 11th of 12 sons

Vital information is necessary and beneficial before we move on. Have you heard about the boy with the multi-colored, technicolored coat? Books, movies, even a Broadway production were created to tell Joseph's story. Before we read or watch those, we should seek the original manuscript for full disclosure of the story. Genesis 37 tells how Joseph ended up in Potiphar's palace.

Jacob's wife, Rachel (see chapter 6 of this book), gave birth to Joseph when God opened her womb. Remember, Jacob had four wives but loved Rachel most. Sticking to this foolish precedent, Jacob favored Joseph over his ten older sons. Foolish turned reckless over time.

The ten older brothers were jealous of the love Jacob evidenced to Joseph. Jealousy turned to hatred, and they responded. One day Jacob sent Joseph to check on his brothers as they were out tending sheep. As they saw Joseph approaching, a plot was planned. It included murder, hiding the evidence, and lying to their father by reporting a ferocious animal attacked his beloved boy.

One of the older brothers couldn't stomach the premeditated murder plan. His proposal included throwing Joseph into a cistern, a deep but dry well in the desert, returning later to rescue him. As Joseph neared, his brothers attacked him, stripped him of the colorful coat, and threw him in the cistern. Moments later a caravan for Egypt approached. A different brother came up with a last-minute idea – sell Joseph to this caravan. So, that's what they did.

When the brothers returned home, they slaughtered a

goat and dipped Joseph's coat in its blood. They took the coat to Jacob for examination. Upon recognition, he believed a wild animal attacked his son and devoured him. Yes, wild did attack and jealous rage devoured, deceiving Jacob. However, as Genesis 37:36 reports, Joseph was sold in Egypt to Potiphar, captain of Pharaoh's guard.

Joseph is not where he should be. Joseph should be with Jacob. Joseph should be tending sheep with his brothers. Instead, years later, Joseph becomes a trusted servant of Potiphar, and as we read in Genesis 39:7, the captain's wife takes notice of Joseph. Dreadful, unpleasant, and shocking things can happen when we're not where we're supposed to be.

A college aged, freshman girl succumbs to peer pressure. She's at a party where she never intended to be, with people whom she never intended to hang, consuming alcohol she never intended to drink. Weeks later she's in a doctor's office receiving words she never intended to hear at this time of life. Her story is not my story, but the outcome is the same – shame from the unintentional, yet real experiences, all because we're not where we're supposed to be.

KEY POINT: RETRACING STEPS, THOUGH DIFFICULT, IS NECESSARY

Taking a mental journey backwards is beneficial to standing unashamed and living as Jesus intends. All too often we struggle to gain answers to the *why* questions regarding shame. Why is this shame so deep? Why won't this shame go away? Why does this shame reappear when I think I've dealt with it? Retracing helps us take responsibility when shame is directly connected to a time when we were where we weren't supposed to be.

However, there are times we're in a place we were never meant to be. Like Joseph, other people's reckless acts land us there. Shame gets accommodated and tolerated in these places as well. Joseph is in Potiphar's house. He's a servant there. And he can't hide or help that he's a well-built and handsome man. Potiphar's wife is in the same house, and she takes notice of

Joseph.

And this is where it goes downhill. Joseph is where he was never supposed to be, and another man's wife takes what she was never supposed to have – a long look at another well-built and handsome man. Premeditated manipulation. Prior to this, if she only struggled with infrequent manipulation out of frustration, this situation would be different. Her actions prove otherwise. A master manipulator is poised to skillfully persuade.

Though Joseph never intended to live in Egypt, as a purchased servant his master deems where he dwells. Genesis 39:2 is comforting to anyone caught in a position or place due to the actions or choices of others. "The Lord was with Joseph..." Though abandoned, God never abandons. Though neglected, God never neglects. Tucking in tight to Jesus is never based on how or where you land; it's trusting in the presence of Jesus in your current reality.

Though his brothers were reckless, God reckoned Joseph's steps. Contrary to abandon and neglect, Jehovah was present and Jehovah provided. Before his wife took notice, Joseph found favor in Potiphar's eyes.

It's one thing to notice a handsome man; *taking* notice takes the look to another level. In the NIV, Genesis 39:7 records, "...his master's wife took notice of Joseph..." The KJV says, "...his master's wife cast her eyes on Joseph..." Casting her eyes literally means she allowed herself to be swept away by what she saw. That, ladies, is way more than noticing a handsome man.

I'm married to a handsome man. Yes, I'm biased, but I'm not blind either. I know when another woman notices my well-built and handsome man, but I'm also aware when she casts her eyes on Kevin, taking notice – taking what doesn't belong to her. Something vigilant rises in me, attentive and aware of her misguided motive. This reaction is not based on jealousy. It's born from covenant.

Potiphar's wife took notice. She cast her eyes on Joseph and in this recorded occurrence was swept away. Clearly, this wasn't her first look. It would take years to earn the trust of

Potiphar. Over time, Potiphar was watching Joseph, and a trust was built. Joseph's integrity earned him the coveted role of overseeing Potiphar's entire household, of everything he owned. Being swept away insinuates she's looked at Joseph many times.

KEY POINT: TAKE WHAT DOESN'T BELONG TO YOU AND YOU'LL GET TAKEN

In Genesis 39:7, Potiphar's wife says to Joseph, "Come to bed with me!" She gets taken, seized by desire. The need to have, the need to be needed, overtook this woman. Noticing a well-built and handsome man swept her away. She was overtaken by a look and demanded this man have sex with her.

Over time she became a woman who was not used to hearing no. Apparently, unreasonable and irrational behavior gets her what she wants, when she wants it. Women like this tend to be spoiled, bratty, snotty, and entitled - character traits fostered from never hearing the word no. This woman says, "jump" and everyone responds, "how high?" In this instant, she has taken her entitled, arrogant, give-me-what-I-want life-style and stooped to a new low – demanding the trusted-by-her-husband, well-built, and handsome man have sex with her.

She is a piece of work. But there's a greater work going on. Joseph is no stranger to being a pawn in the game of manipulation. His brothers maneuvered him in their manipulating plot in an attempt to simmer their jealousy. Yet, Joseph wouldn't allow their plotting antics to injure his integrity. A lesson he remembered and relied on is in this recent incident.

Genesis 39:8 says, "But he refused." That's powerful proof Joseph is willing to stand up and confront a manipulator. And he gives solid reasoning. Potiphar trusts Joseph and makes him in charge of the entire household. Joseph says, "Everything he owns he has entrusted to my care. No one is greater in this house than I am. My master has withheld nothing from me except you, because you are his wife."

Integrity takes responsibility and does the right thing.

Integrity drives his refusal to get tangled in her manipulating wiles. InteGRITy has grit - determination, fortitude, tenacity. Joseph was predetermined and ready with a response. He didn't stammer and sputter as a manipulating woman made her demands. Joseph had fortitude. I like this word. When on the receiving end of manipulation, Joseph had the emotional strength to face his manipulator.

Oh, to be tenacious like Joseph. If a manipulator is one thing, it's stubborn. Tenacity must be a step higher. It doesn't back down – it firmly and stubbornly adheres to a purpose. Potiphar's wife has her will set – she wants Joseph in her bed, and she wants him now. The grit Joseph shows in this temptation is tenacious – he is unwilling to yield, he can't be controlled, he won't be persuaded.

Manipulators hate integrity and grit. But there's something more powerful and steadfast than grit guiding Joseph's life – righteousness. Joseph adds a crucial question to this confrontation: "How then could I do such a wicked thing and sin against God?"

A follower of Jesus is mastered by Him. A master manipulator has no control over you – unless you allow it. Righteousness is the only way Joseph remained firm in refusal. Psalm 23:3 says, "You lead me in paths of righteousness." Following implies a leader is present. Joseph is being led by God. Genesis 39:2 continues, "...the Lord was with Joseph and he prospered." Joseph prospers in this moment because righteousness is his path. Integrity guides all. Righteousness leads followers of Jesus in the right direction.

Stepping off the path of righteousness was more disconcerting to Joseph than being manipulated by a wild woman. It's easy to look at Potiphar's wife and see crazy – that's a level of manipulation most woman will never see or become. But what about that woman you saw in the mirror? She must come to grips with her personal participation in manipulation.

KEY POINT: INTEGRITY + RIGHTEOUSNESS = UNASHAMED

Examine yourself. How's your integrity? How do you do at taking responsibility and doing the right thing? What's your grit level? Determination, fortitude, and tenacity are requirements needed to have integrity.

I had a co-worker who was a manipulator. And he was a master at it. As a new staff member, I saw right through this guy's wiles. Because we worked on a staff that had an overarching goal it was necessary to meet, sharing ideas and plans under our areas of responsibility. In our very first meeting together, I saw through his manipulation. After I laid out my short-term goals he said, "That'll never work." That was the last time we met.

My response to him went something like this: "Well, _____ (integrity says I can't use his name), apparently you've used that line on others since it rolled off your tongue so easily. How about this? I'm keeping to my goals. Your blatant negativity and manipulation can't and won't work on me."

Did I mention we were on a ministry staff together? That should have meant paths of righteousness were tread by all. His manipulation continued. As a master, his arsenal was bottomless. One day he came to me reporting a woman left the church because of something I was overheard saying at an event I hadn't attended. Yes, you read that correctly. I wasn't present, but I was *heard* gossiping about this woman. He didn't know I wasn't there, so he took what he heard and spread it like wildfire, attempting to manipulate and ruin my reputation as a staff member.

He stood in the doorway of my office, hands spread across the threshold like I was trapped inside. Looking down on me as I sat at my desk, he waited for a response. What I wanted to do and what I did are different. Integrity and righteousness were my guide. Good thing, because if Ellen was in control he'd have two eyeballs rolling on the floor.

I simply turned to the desk phone and began dialing. Mid-dial, he asked, "Who are you calling?" I respond, "_____" (Insert the name of the woman I was heard gossiping about.) He replied, "You can't do that." "Well, _____, yes, I can, and you can't stop me. So please, back out of my door and leave. Our conversation is done."

A red face. I've never seen a man's face turn that red, that fast. "I'm telling you, you are not allowed to make that phone call," he spewed. I continued dialing and waited for someone to answer on the other end. She answered the phone, he bolted, and I got to the bottom of why she left the church. It had nothing to do with me – it was a personal matter involving her daughter who lived in a different community and needed her mom.

His manipulating (and the red on his face) went to new levels. This book could be filled with examples I personally experienced from this man – who had successfully manipulated others in this church for years. Many people were aware, but they chose to avoid rather than confront. Righteousness was my chosen path, and those who walk it are led by God's ways. Choosing this path wouldn't allow me to jab him in the eye or punch him in the face, otherwise, I'd be doing a wicked thing and sinning against God.

Righteousness doesn't need to get even. Righteousness doesn't involve rights. For a lot of women, this is a sticking point. Perhaps you've told another or been told that you have the right to a voice; you should be heard. On an earthly level, this may be true, even necessary for order and systems (workplace, community, family) to function at their best and be most productive. On a spiritual level what rights do we have? Search the Bible. What rights do you find? I found one – there may be more, but I couldn't find them. John 1:12 says, "To all who receive Jesus, who believe in His name, He gave the right to become children of God."

When I desperately want to be heard – *hey! I have something to say here* – no one seems to be listening, I need to take notice of my path. The way of Ellen always wants and believes she has the right to be heard and demands others listen. When walking on paths of righteousness, I desire to follow God's ways, His way. If I'm intently listening to His voice, what I feel I have to say is a distant sound, not as important and not in control of my emotions and behavior.

Joseph refuses Potiphar's wife because he's on the path of righteousness. But he didn't refuse her once. Genesis 39:10 says, "Though she spoke to Joseph day after day, he refused to go to bed with her or even be with her." A scorned, manipulative woman is erratic, and like a volcano, unpredictable. Joseph is firmly rooted to no, and she's about to blow.

Saying no is one thing, but refusing to be in the same room is another. It's no longer just about her desiring sex. Now she's been refused, ignored, and dissed in front of the entire household, and she views that as deplorable. No one will get away with refusing, ignoring, and dissing her. Now she must dig deep into her manipulative arsenal and take her best shot at Joseph.

Genesis 39:11-12 records, "One day he went into the house to attend to his duties and none of the household servants was inside..." Gee, how did everyone leave this palace house at the exact same time, leaving Potiphar's wife all by herself?

"...she caught him by his cloak..." An assault by surprise!

"...and said, 'come to bed with me!'..." She's attempting to weaken his integrity and knock him off his path of righteousness. Incidentally, no one has the power or ability to knock you off a path – they can try, persuade, sway, or manipulate but stepping off is your choice.

"...but he left his cloak in her hand and ran out of the house." The path of righteousness led Joseph right out of his robe. He was more concerned with his character than his cloak. She literally took matters into her own hands, seizing hold of his outer robe while attempting to physically manipulate Joseph to suit her own purposes. Not only did he refuse her sexual advances, he refused to be manipulated. Oh, she's manipulating, but it only comes to fruition if he falls for it.

KEY POINT: RESPOND WELL WHEN YOU CAN'T HAVE WHAT YOU WANT

What do you want but can't have? A clean house, new car, bigger diamond, more stuff? You want something but you don't get it - a husband who understands your needs, a friend who will listen, a calm boss, better behaved kids? How do you attempt to get the things you want?

Do you expect others to adjust or change to suit you...your desires, your wants, what you feel you're entitled to? How have you manipulated others or circumstances to get what you want? It takes careful inspection – the kind of examination only the Holy Spirit can truly reveal.

Areas of your heart could be accommodating shame from not responding well when you can't have what you want. Ask the Light of the World to reveal these hidden yet damaging places. And if you've struggled with manipulation, invite Jesus to settle in and renovate the spaces of your heart affected by its mastery. If manipulation isn't stopped, it continues its destructive path, and you end up tolerating and accommodating shame left in its wake.

Genesis 39:13-15 describes how she blames Joseph for coming onto her. She still holds the cloak he ran out of – her proof Joseph came to her with sexual intentions. Holding his cloak looked bad for Joseph – but that's just circumstantial evidence. Running with his character still intact proves Joseph is firmly rooted on the path of righteousness. But that doesn't mean Potiphar will believe him.

In Genesis 39:16-20, the master manipulator creates a story as it's rolling off her tongue and tells it to her husband, "...that slave you brought us came to me to make sport of me, but as soon as I screamed, he left his cloak beside me and ran...this is how your slave treated me..." She blames her husband for Joseph being there. Potiphar forgets Joseph's integrity and believes his manipulating wife. Potiphar burns with anger and places Joseph in prison, all because a woman's manipulation didn't get her what she wanted.

When a woman is consumed with her unmet appetite, she may resort to manipulation and people are sure to get hurt. Joseph is in prison – the same guy whose brothers wanted him dead but instead sold him to strangers - is now unfairly in prison. He doesn't deserve this; he didn't do anything wrong.

KEY POINT: WHEN LIFE IS UNFAIR, SEEK A FAITHFUL GOD

The Kevin Harbin family does not dwell in a fair house. Never have, never will. Ask any of our six children, even the adult ones who have homes of their own, if they grew up in a fair house and they'll respond, "Never!" If I wanted to give one a piece of gum and not another, I did. If Kevin took one, and not another, for a daddy/donut date, it was accepted. If one stayed up late, the others went to bed on time. No screaming, no yelling, no unjust emotions allowed. Just because one received a driver's license at sixteen didn't mean they all would. We never made sure equal amounts were spent on gifts or equal time spent with each one. The Harbin house is simply not a fair house.

But one thing remains consistent in our home. One thing our kids can count on is prayer. Kevin and I pray for and with our kids. Always have, always will. From the first day our eldest left for kindergarten, we prayed. Every single school morning since 1996, we stand near the door they'll vacate, we hold hands, and we pray. At times tears are involved. On occasion, a breath separates raised voices to calmly state, "Ok, it's time to pray."

Though four have left the nest, praying for them remains. Just earlier today, as Kevin and I spent alone time at our summer place, we prayed specifically for each of our six kids. Inviting God into their lives, seeking God on their behalf, taking their burdens to Jesus, and laying their problems at His feet never grows old.

We want our kids to know God is at the center of the Harbin House. When life isn't fair, God will be there. When we're deceived, feeling half-hearted, victimized, in doubt, stressed, disappointed and desperate, mistreated, or manipulated, God is trustworthy. We don't need a fair existence; we need a faithful God.

Genesis 39:20-21, 23 "...while Joseph was in prison, the Lord was with him, showed him kindness, and granted him favor...the Lord was with Joseph and gave him success in whatever he did." Joseph went from the palace to the prison, accused of something he didn't do. That's true. Be careful not to ignore or gloss over theses five words *the Lord was with Joseph*.

God didn't freak out when Joseph was caught in a manipulative woman's wake. He never abandoned Joseph when his brothers threw him in a pit. He wasn't unaware when Joseph landed in prison. God was always there. And Joseph recognized His presence. Even as a manipulative woman was seeking to ruin his reputation and injure his integrity, Joseph trusted God and knew His existence reigned over any situation Joseph faced.

Potiphar's wife was filled with shame as she manipulated a palace of people. Joseph was free of shame even though he was locked up in a prison cell.

Your circumstances or situations do not give shame permission to be accommodated in your heart. Shame does not need to be tolerated in your life. Not ever!

Regardless of your current reality, allow Jesus to gain access to every nook and cranny of your soul and shed His light where shame has been accommodated and tolerated. And like Joseph, you can be freed from the prison of shame.

Isn't it time to reclaim the spaces in your heart where shame has been accommodated and tolerated? Shame is a name-changer, desiring to keep the shame game alive. But Jesus is the game-changer, waiting to take up residence where shame once resided.

In Genesis 50:20 Joseph speaks words everyone can claim as their own - to stand unashamed and living as Jesus intends. When shame comes knocking at your heart's door deceiving you, it must be tolerated and accommodated. Aim Joseph's words at it, "You intended to harm me, but God intended it for good..."

Unashamed does not leave us unscathed or unaffected from problems, crises, or trouble. Joseph had problems, he lived through crisis, and he certainly knew trouble. But he also had a

Holy God with him though it all. Joseph could separate the intentional harm done to him from the intentional love of a good and Holy God. Joseph stood firm when he made a distinction of the harm from the holy in his life.

We can stand unashamed when Jesus resides and abides in our hearts. He desires to take up residence in all the places, even the hidden spaces, allowing shame no access. A heart wholly owned and operated by Jesus leaves no room for holes where shame imbeds.

As Joseph separated the intentional harm others inflicted on him from the intentional love God had for him, we must separate the shame we tolerate and accommodate from the Savior who deeply desires to invade every space in our hearts.

Shame intends to harm; Jesus intends to save.

Shame intends chaos; Jesus intends peace.

Shame intends defeat; Jesus intends victory.

Allow Jesus total access to your life. He intentionally died and God intentionally rose the dead to life so you could stand unashamed.

PONDER

deeply, carefully, and thoughtfully consider

1. Carefully but honestly describe yourself. Are you the noun or the verb: a manipulator or one who manipulates? What's the difference?

2. Integrity lives right. On a scale of 1-5 with 1 being hardly ever and 5 being most of the time, what's your level of determination, fortitude, and tenacity?

3. Righteousness doesn't involve rights. Does this have you stuck? Explain.

PERSUADE
God's Word influences, encourages, and guides

1. Joseph refused to sin against God. Read Jeremiah
   6:15. *They have no shame at all; they do not even
   know how to blush.* How are you influenced by this
   passage? Read on in Jeremiah 6:16. What verbs are
   used to encourage one to stand unashamed?

2. Joseph ran out of his robe with righteousness
   intact. [Genesis 39:12] How do the following verses
   influence and encourage you to be guided by
   righteousness?

   [a] 1Samuel 26:23

   [b] Psalm 33:5

   [c] Psalm 48:10

   [d] Psalm 89:14

   [e] Proverbs 11:8

   [f] Hosea 10:12

   [g] Amos 5:24

   [h] Zephaniah 2:3

PRACTICAL
applying Biblical Truth to present day

1. A manipulative woman couldn't get what she wanted, her schemes attempted to ruin Joseph, landing him in prison. Through it all, the Lord was with Joseph. Has a certain shame manipulated you? Has it deceived you that God isn't there or doesn't care? Apply Genesis 39:2 – it was a reality and a promise for Joseph *before* manipulation entered his life.

2. Potiphar's wife behaved badly when she couldn't have what she wanted. Is contentment a struggle for you? How can you apply 1Timothy 6:6 to this struggle?

3. Jesus says in Matthew 6:33, *"But seek first His kingdom and His righteousness..."* Apply this directive from Jesus to your contentment level.

PERSONAL
inviting Jesus into your current reality

1. Joseph was unfairly imprisoned, yet a faithful God was present. *We don't need a fair existence, we need a faithful God*, Ellen writes. Describe where shame has you screaming, "Unfair!"

2. Jesus is ready and waiting to take up residence in every space and place of your heart where shame dwells. Don't wait any longer - invite Him to invade your prison of shame and begin to STAND unashamed and live as Jesus intends! Write a prayer releasing the shame holding you captive.

CONCLUSION

They're gone! The warts are gone. God said it would happen. One day, He spoke quietly to my heart and said as soon as this book was completed, they'd start to disappear. As soon as chapter eight was finished – the very week it was done - the pesky bumps, that for months had taken up residence on half of my digits, began disappearing. For months, the dermatologist did everything she could to help but to no avail. As I said, it's a virus my immune system was slow to attack. Looking back, God didn't give me warts, but He sure used them to help me understand how shame affects hearts.

Salicylic acid, duct tape, cryotherapy, laser treatment, vinegar, over-the-counter compounds, antibiotics, and a pharmaceutical cream were all tried but failed to alleviate the warts. No one or nothing is to blame. The warts remained – I needed them. The pain, the agony, the embarrassment, and the unsuccessful treatments taught me valuable lessons.

The harm and assault of shame is painful, agonizing, and embarrassing. There is truly only one remedy, one answer, one solution for shame that stands above them all – Jesus. Until we're done breathing air, problems, crises, and trouble aren't going anywhere. Since shame continues to remain in this world, it no longer needs to reign in your heart, ruling your emotions, actions, and thoughts.

Jesus took our shame to His cross; therefore, it is not our shackle. Paul is a man chained to a prison wall – that's a problem, a crisis, and big trouble. Shame is knocking at his heart's door. But Paul says in Philippians chapter one "...being confident...he who began a good work will carry it on to completion...I eagerly expect and hope that I will in **no way be ashamed**, but have sufficient courage...whatever happens, conduct yourselves in a manner worthy of the gospel of Christ, then...I will know that you **stand firm**..."

Tolerating and allowing shame trips us up and knocks us down. Like Paul, we must also be confident God began a good work in us, and He is faithful to carry it to completion. When shame knocks on your heart's door, whatever is happening in your life, will you have sufficient courage to conduct yourself worthy of the gospel, in no way ashamed, and standing firm in your faith?

Send an email to ellen@ellenharbin.com

...if you'd like to keep updated when future volumes in this series are published

...if you're interested in having Ellen speak at your women's retreat or conference

...if you'd like to have Ellen as a guest (via SKYPE, fb live, or a phone call) at your *STAND unashamed* Bible Study

...if you'd like to discuss bringing the STAND women's conference to your church or geographic location

ABOUT THE AUTHOR

Ellen Harbin is a gifted Bible teacher and conference speaker, creatively applying the truth of God's Word to all of life's triumphs and challenges. She is also the founder of the STAND Women's Conference, debuting fall of 2017 in SE Michigan. She's engaging and inspiring; guiding and encouraging women to take a closer look at their relationship with Jesus and live life as He intends.

Ellen is married to Kevin and lives in southeast Michigan. They have six children - four biological and two through adoption, and three daughters-in-law.

Ellen likes dating her man and being with her family. Laughing hard, reading, deep conversations, spontaneity, sunrises, and quality time with friends are highlights in life – adding coffee to all is an added bonus.

Ellen says being a follower of Jesus is the absolute best decision of her life.

Made in the USA
Columbia, SC
25 October 2017